Longman Practice Exam Papers

GCSE Biology

Chris Millican

Series editors
Geoff Black and Stuart Wall

Titles available for GCSE

Biology
Chemistry
Mathematics (Intermediate)
Mathematics (Higher)
Physics
Science

Addison Wesley Longman Ltd, Edinburgh Gate, Harlow, CM20 2JE, England
and Associated Companies throughout the World

© Addison Wesley Longman 1998

All rights reserved; no part of this publication may be reproduced, stored in a retrieval system, or transmitted in any form or by any means, electronic, mechanical, photocopying, recording or otherwise without either the prior written consent of the Publishers or a licence permitting restricted copying in the United Kingdom issued by the Copyright Licensing Agency Ltd, 90 Tottenham Court Road, London, W1P 9HE.

First published 1998

ISBN 0 582 35644-X

British Library Cataloguing-in-Publication Data
A catalogue record for this book is available from the British Library.

Set in 11/13pt Times

Printed in Great Britain by Henry Ling Ltd, at The Dorset Press, Dorchester, Dorset.

Contents

Editors' preface   iv

Acknowledgements   iv

How to use this book   1

Paper 1 level   2

Paper 2 level   13

Paper 3 level   26

Solutions to practice exam papers   38

How well did you do?   54

Editors' Preface

Longman Practice Exam Papers are written by experienced GCSE examiners and teachers. They will provide you with an ideal opportunity to practise under exam-type conditions before your actual school or college mocks or before the GCSE examination itself. As well as becoming familiar with the vital skill of pacing yourself through a whole exam paper, you can check your answers against examiner solutions and mark-schemes to assess the level you have reached.

Longman Practice Exam Papers can be used alongside the *Longman GCSE Study Guides* and *Longman Exam Practice Kits* to provide a comprehensive range of home study support as you prepare to take your GCSE in each subject covered.

Acknowledgements

Thanks to Clive Hurford for all his help with the preparation of this manuscript.

How to use this book

- Find a quiet place to work, and make sure that you have enough time to attempt the whole paper.
- Make sure you have the right equipment ready; pencils, pens, rubber, ruler, calculator (with a new battery).
- Carefully read the instructions at the beginning of the paper.
- Look at the number of questions to be answered, and make a rough plan of your time.
- Read each question at least twice. It's a shame to answer the wrong question, as you won't get the marks you deserve. You might want to underline key words.
- Look at the number of lines and number of marks available to decide the amount of detail needed.
- In calculations, show clearly how you work out your answer. Show each stage of the calculation and remember to state the units.
- Work steadily through the paper, and keep an eye on the time, checking your progress every 30 minutes.
- Attempt all of the questions. If you get stuck, come back to that question later.
- Don't stop! If you finish early, go back and check that you have completed all the questions and check that you haven't made any errors.
- If you run out of time, be sensible and keep your answers clear and readable. Remember that it is usually easier to get the first few marks on a question than to continue trying to get the last few harder marks on another question.
- If a question asks you to label a diagram, make sure that the label line is pointing exactly at the part you have identified.

Using these practice exam papers

This book contains 3 exam papers set at the **Higher level**. They each contain 10 questions, and include the more difficult syllabus topics which would allow you to achieve grades **A*–D**.

- The answers and mark-schemes to these papers are given at the end of the papers. Use these to check your answers **after** you have attempted to answer the questions to the best of your ability. Try to answer all the questions – do not give up too easily.

Longman Examination Board

General Certificate of Secondary Education
Biology
Paper 1

Time: 90 minutes

Instructions

- Answer all questions in the spaces provided in this exam paper.
- Show all stages in any calculations, and state the units. You may use a calculator if you wish.
- Include diagrams in your answers where these are helpful.

Information for candidates

- The marks for various parts of questions are shown in brackets, e.g. (1 mark).
- This exam paper has 10 questions.
- You are allowed 90 minutes for this paper.
- The maximum mark for this paper is 100.

Number	Mark
1.	
2.	
3.	
4.	
5.	
6.	
7.	
8.	
9.	
10.	

---

1. (a) Complete the passage about cell division by filling in the missing words.

   Inside the .... of every cell are chromosomes which carry genetic information. The chromosomes are made of a chemical called .... Inside a human body cell, the number of chromosomes is .... When the cell is about to divide, the chromosomes copy themselves (replicate) so that each daughter cell gets a set of chromosomes. There are two types of cell division, ... and .... In .... the number of chromosomes is the same as the number in the original cell; we call this the .... number. In the other type of cell division, the daughter cell has half as many chromosomes as the original cell. We say that the daughter cell is .... This type of cell division occurs when .... are being formed.

   (9 marks)

   Leave margin blank

(b) Look at the diagrams showing the stages of cell division.

A   B   C   D   E

(i) Put the stages into the correct order. **(1 mark)**

☐☐☐☐☐

(ii) Which type of cell division is this?

....

(1 mark)

(iii) Give one reason for your answer to part (ii).

....

(1 mark)
Total: 12 marks

2. (a) (i) Which gas is produced in photosynthesis?

....

(ii) Which gas is produced in respiration?

....

(2 marks)

(b) Bicarbonate indicator changes colour depending on the amount of carbon dioxide present.

Yellow ◄─────────── Red ───────────► Purple
Lots of carbon dioxide   Normal amount of carbon dioxide   Very little carbon dioxide

Five tubes were set up as shown in the diagram. Each one contained red bicarbonate indicator and they were left for 4 hours.

A — bicarbonate indicator, pondweed — LIGHT
B — pond snails — LIGHT
C — LIGHT
D — DARK
E — LIGHT

Complete the table to show what colour you would expect the indicator to be in each tube, and suggest an explanation for your answer.

Turn over

Tube	Colour of bicarbonate indicator after 4 hours	Explanation
A		
B		
C		
D		
E		

(10 marks)
Total: 12 marks

3. The diagram shows the inheritance of a genetic disease in one family.

   (a) (i) Is the allele causing this disease dominant or recessive?................................ **(1 mark)**

   How can you tell? ....

   .... **(1 mark)**

   (ii) Is the allele causing this disease sex-linked? .... **(1 mark)**

   How can you tell? ....

   .... **(1 mark)**

   (b) Use the symbols **D** and **d** for the gene controlling this disease.
   What would the genotypes of individuals 1 and 2 be?

   1 .... 2 .... **(2 marks)**

   (c) This disease matches the pattern of inheritance shown by one of the following diseases.

         Haemophilia   Cystic fibrosis   Huntington's disease

   Identify the correct disease and underline your answer. **(1 mark)**
   Total: 7 marks

4. Barley seeds contain stored starch to provide energy when the seed starts to germinate. The seed also contains the enzyme amylase to break down the starch.

(a) When starch is broken down by amylase, what product is formed?

.... **(1 mark)**

(b) Four barley seeds were treated as shown, then placed cut-side down on some agar jelly containing starch, and left for 12 hours.

A – seed cut in half then placed on agar jelly

B – seed cut in half, boiled for 5 minutes, then placed on agar jelly

C – seed cut in half, soaked in acid for 5 minutes, then placed on agar jelly

D – seed not cut in half, but placed on agar jelly intact

After 12 hours, iodine was poured over the surface of the agar jelly.

(i) What colour would you see if starch was present?

.... **(1 mark)**

The diagram shows how the agar jelly looked at this stage.

(ii) Suggest an explanation for each of the results shown.

A ....

....

.... **(1 mark)**

B ....

....

.... **(1 mark)**

C ....

....

.... **(1 mark)**

D ....

....

.... **(1 mark)**

Turn over

(iii) Maize seeds contain less amylase than barley seeds. Describe what you would see if you repeated step A with a maize seed.

....

.... **(2 marks)**
Total: 8 marks

5. The diagram shows a section through the spinal cord.

   (a) Complete the diagram to show a reflex arc, by drawing and labelling the three neurones involved.

   relay neurone   motor neurone   sensory neurone   **(3 marks)**

   (b) What is the name given to a junction between two neurones?

   .... **(1 mark)**

   (c) Complete the table about reflex actions. The first line has been done for you.   **(4 marks)**

Name of reflex	Stimulus	Response
withdrawal reflex	pain, e.g. hot object touches skin	muscle contracts to move the body away from the stimulus
		pupil decreases in size
	food or liquid in the trachea	

   (d) Give one difference between a reflex action and a voluntary action.

   ....

   ....

   (1 marks)
   Total: 9 marks

6. Humans have carried out breeding programmes so that the wheat we have today is very different from wild wheat. This is called **selective breeding**, and it has led to improved varieties being developed. The diagram shows wild wheat and modern wheat which has been developed by selective breeding.

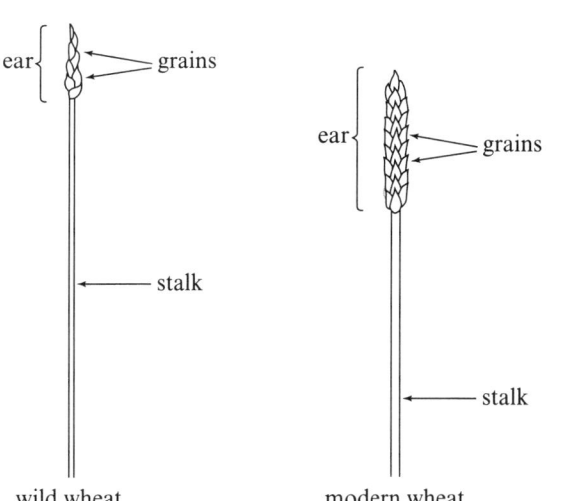

wild wheat   modern wheat

(a) Choose two differences between the types of wheat that you can see in the diagram and explain how each of them would be of benefit to humans.

Difference ....

How it benefits humans...

.... **(1 mark)**

Difference ....

How it benefits humans...

.... **(1 mark)**

(b) Suggest a third difference, which you cannot see in the diagrams, that would benefit humans.

Difference .... **(1 mark)**

How it benefits humans...

.... **(1 mark)**

(c) Once a successful variety has been developed by selective breeding, why would it be an advantage if the plant could be cloned, rather than allowed to reproduce sexually?

....

....

....

(2 marks)
Total: 6 marks

Turn over

7. This is a diagram of the human respiratory system.

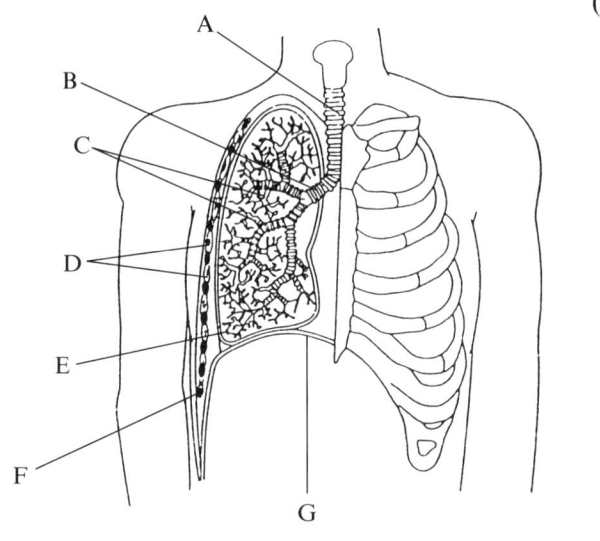

(a) Which letter represents the part where

   (i) gas exchange occurs? ....

   (ii) there are rings of cartilage?

   ....

   (iii) muscles contract when the person breathes in?

   .... and ....

(3 marks)

(b) The diagram below shows an alveolus and the blood vessel close to it.

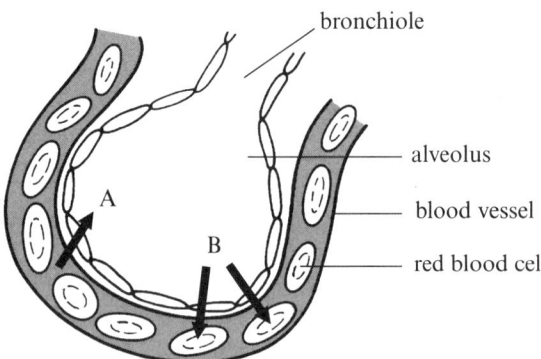

   (i) Which type of blood vessel is shown?

   ....

(1 mark)

   (ii) What are the two gases A and B?

   A .... B .... **(2 marks)**

   (iii) Which process in the body produces gas A?

   ....

(1 mark)

   (iv) How do gases A and B move between the alveolus and the blood?

   ....

(1 mark)

Leave margin blank

(c) This diagram shows a model which is sometimes used to demonstrate ventilation of the lungs.

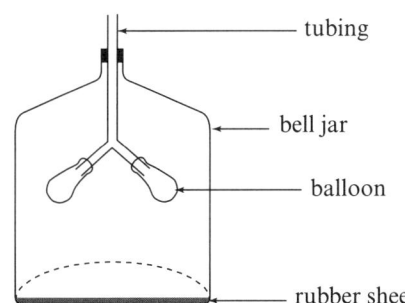

(i) Name the parts of the human respiratory system represented by the following parts of the model:

balloons ....

rubber sheet ....

bell jar ....

(3 marks)

(ii) If you push the rubber sheet upwards (as shown by the dotted line in the diagram), what happens to the balloons?

....

(1 mark)

(iii) Explain this by referring to volume changes and pressure changes inside the bell jar.

....

....

....

(3 marks)
Total: 16 marks

8. The graph shows the level of two sex hormones at different stages of the menstrual cycle in a woman who is not pregnant. The cycle lasts 28 days.

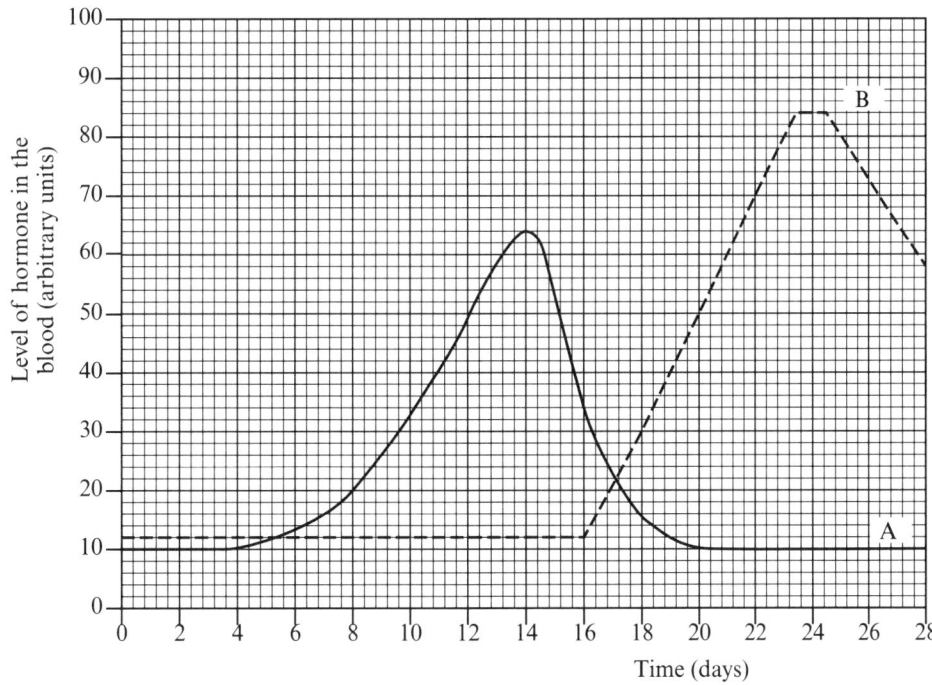

(a) On which day of the menstrual cycle would

(i) ovulation occur? ....

(ii) menstruation start? .... **(2 marks)**

Turn over

(b) Identify hormones A and B.

A .... B .... **(2 marks)**

(c) (i) Which hormone, A or B, is produced in large amounts during pregnancy?

.... **(1 mark)**

(ii) Which organ secretes this hormone during pregnancy?

.... **(1 mark)**

(d) The diagram shows the foetus during pregnancy.

Choose one of the parts labelled with a letter, and state how it protects the foetus from harm during pregnancy.

Letter ....

How it protects the foetus

....

....

....

....
(1 mark)
Total: 7 marks

9. The diagram shows a section through the human heart.

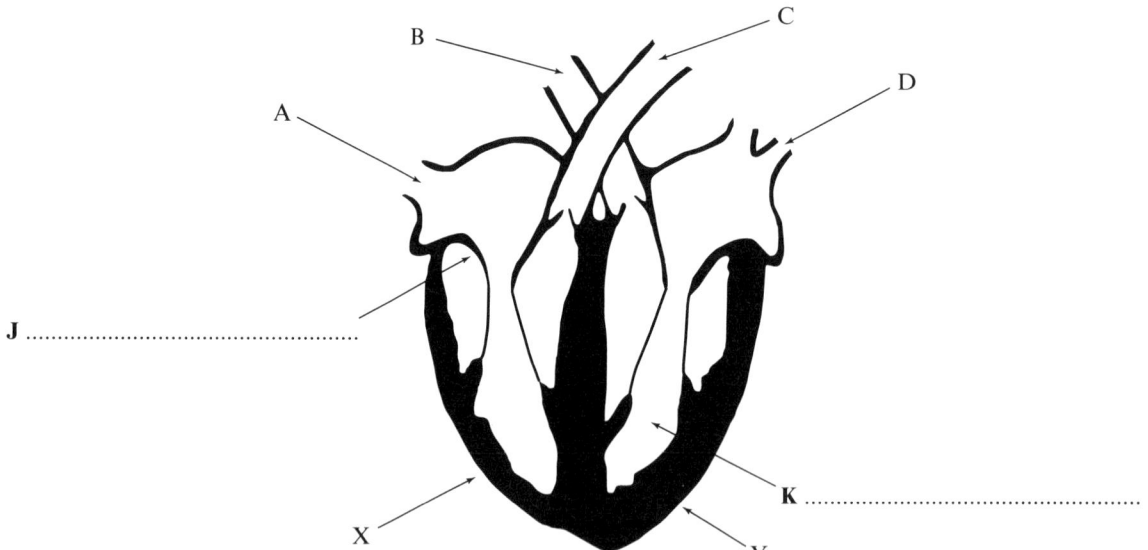

(a) (i) Label the parts of the heart indicated by **J** and **K** in the diagram. **(2 marks)**

(ii) Add arrows to show the movement of oxygenated blood through the heart. Do not show how deoxygenated blood moves. **(1 mark)**

(b) Which of the blood vessels A, B, C, or D

   (i) is carrying deoxygenated blood to the lungs?..

   (ii) is carrying blood at the highest pressure? .... **(2 marks)**

(c) (i) What type of tissue is X? .... **(1 mark)**

   (ii) Explain why Y is thicker than X.

   ....

   ....
   (2 marks)

(d) Coronary arteries bring blood carrying food and oxygen to the heart muscle. The diagram shows a coronary artery from a person with heart disease.

   (i) What type of substance is Q?

   ....
   (1 mark)

   (ii) If the artery continues to be blocked, what could happen to this person?

   ....
   (1 mark)

   (iii) Suggest two factors which may cause heart disease, or make it worse.

   ....

   ....
   (2 marks)
   Total: 12 marks

Turn over

10. The graph shows the effect of releasing untreated sewage into a river at point X.

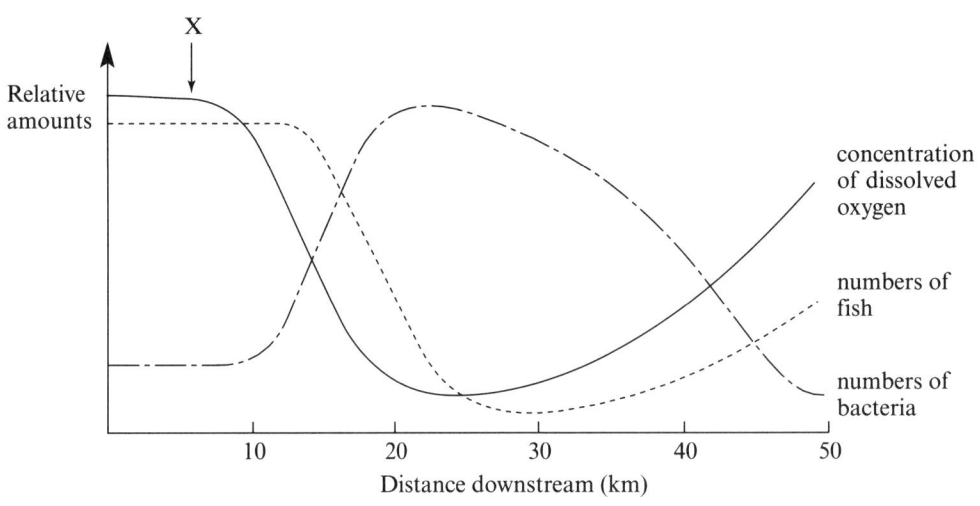

(a) Explain, giving reasons:
  (i) the changes in the numbers of bacteria

  ....
  ....
  ....
  (3 marks)

  (ii) the changes in the dissolved oxygen levels

  ....
  ....
  (2 marks)

  (iii) the changes in the number of fish

  ....
  ....
  (2 marks)

(b) Mark with a Y the point on the graph at which the numbers of bacteria return to normal.
  (1 mark)

(c) Sewage contains a lot of urea. Bacteria in the water change this into nitrate.
  (i) How will this affect the growth of algae in the river?

  ....
  (1 mark)

  (ii) What problem could this cause after 10 to 20 days?

  ....
  ....
  (2 marks)
  Total: 11 marks

Longman Examination Board

General Certificate of Secondary Education
Biology
Paper 2

Time: 90 minutes

Instructions

- Answer all questions in the spaces provided in this exam paper.
- Show all stages in any calculations, and state the units. You may use a calculator if you wish.
- Include diagrams in your answers where these are helpful.

Information for candidates

- The marks for various parts of questions are shown in brackets, e.g. (1 mark).
- This exam paper has 10 questions.
- You are allowed 90 minutes for this paper.
- The maximum mark for this paper is 100.

Number	Mark
1.	
2.	
3.	
4.	
5.	
6.	
7.	
8.	
9.	
10.	

---

1. Some visking tubing was stretched across the neck of a thistle funnel, and a strong salt solution was poured into the funnel. The level of the salt solution was marked, then the funnel was immersed in water as shown.

   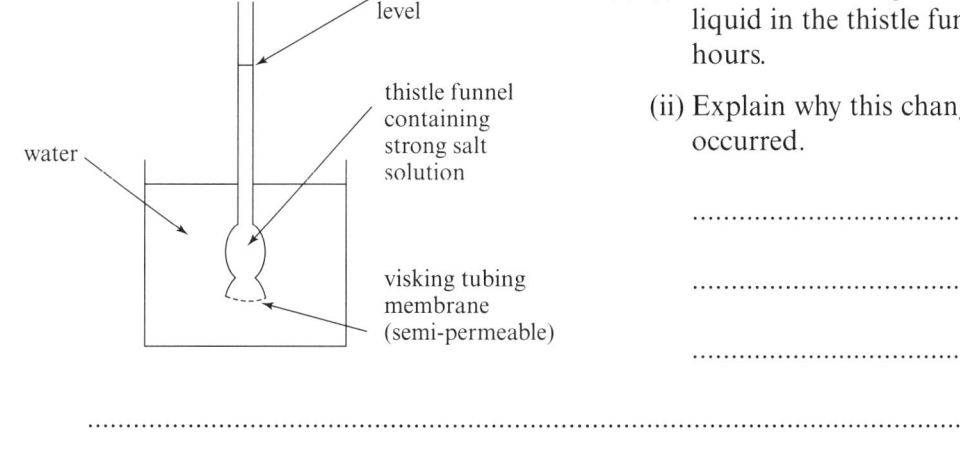

   (a) (i) Mark on the diagram the level of liquid in the thistle funnel after two hours. **(1 mark)**

   (ii) Explain why this change has occurred.

   ....

   ....

   ....

   ....

   ....

   (2 marks)

Leave margin blank

13 **Turn over**

(b) (i) If plant cells had been immersed in water, which of these diagrams shows what the plant cells would look like? .... **(1 mark)**

    A   B   C

(ii) How would you describe this plant cell?

....

(1 mark)

(iii) Which part of the cell has the same function as the visking tubing in the experiment?

....

(1 mark)
Total: 6 marks

2. The diagram shows part of a section through a leaf.

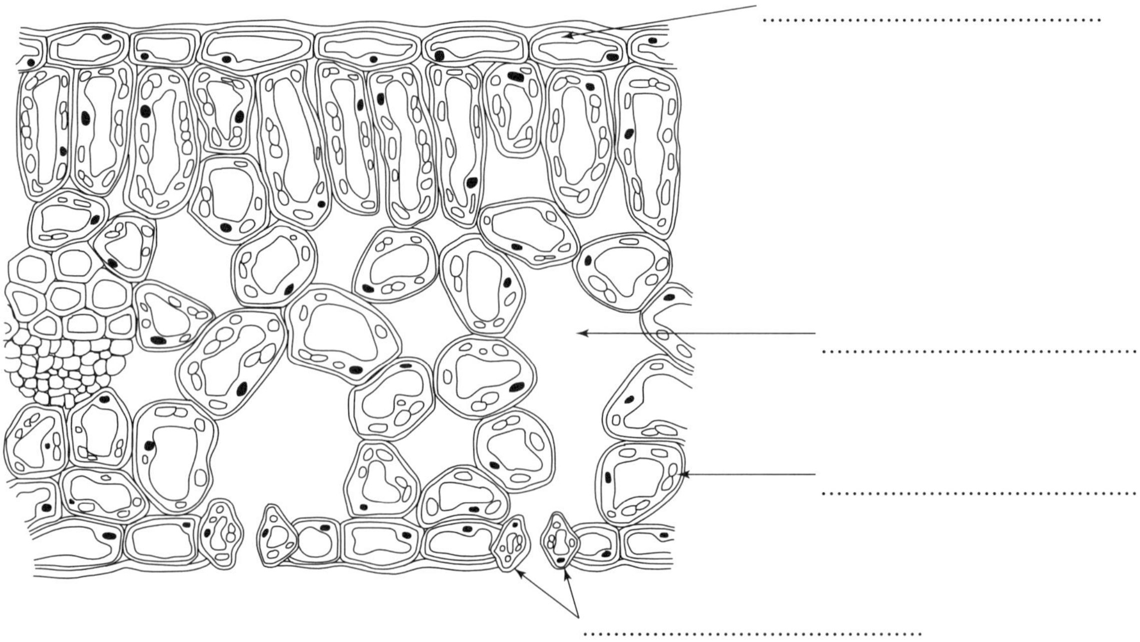

(a) (i) Label the parts indicated. **(4 marks)**
   (ii) Mark with an X the part of the cell responsible for trapping light. **(1 mark)**
   (iii) Which gas is produced in photosynthesis?

....

(1 mark)

   (iv) Mark with a Y the place where this gas escapes from the leaf. **(1 mark)**

(b) A class did an experiment to find out which colour of light caused the fastest rate of photosynthesis.

Five leaf discs were cut from leaves, and placed in water containing dissolved sodium hydrogen carbonate. A coloured light was shone on to the leaf discs so they would photosynthesise. As gas escaped from the leaf discs, they floated to the surface of the tube, and the average time for the leaf discs to float was recorded.
The experiment was then repeated using different colours of light.

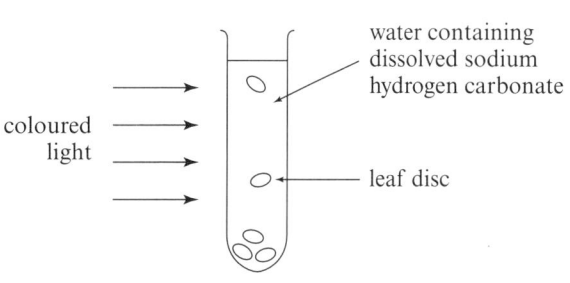

Colour of light	Average time taken for leaf discs to float (minutes)
violet	6
blue	3
green	12
yellow	11
red	4

(i) Plot these results as a bar chart. **(3 marks)**

(ii) Which colour of light causes the fastest rate of photosynthesis?

....

(1 mark)

Turn over

(iii) Why was sodium hydrogen carbonate dissolved in the water?

....

....

(2 marks)

(iv) Why were five leaf discs used in each tube, instead of one?

....

(1 mark)

(v) State two ways the class could make sure they carried out a fair test.

....

....

(2 marks)
Total: 16 marks

3. Add the appropriate word to match each of the definitions given. This question is related to cell division and genetics.

   (a) (i) .... An individual with two identical alleles for a particular feature.

   (ii) .... A cell with half the normal number of chromosomes.

   (iii) .... An allele which always shows in the phenotype, no matter which other allele is present with it.

   (iv) .... A condition which is more common in males than females, because the gene controlling it is carried on the X-chromosome.

   (4 marks)

   (b) In pea plants, the flower colour is controlled by genes. The allele for purple flowers (F) is dominant to the allele for white flowers (f).

   (i) Tick the correct boxes in the table to show which phenotypes would be found in the offspring of crosses A, B and C. **(3 marks)**

		Phenotypes of offspring	
Cross	Genotypes of parents	Plants with purple flowers	Plants with white flowers
A	FF × FF		
B	Ff × ff		
C	Ff × Ff		
D			✓

   (ii) What would be the genotypes of the parent plants in cross D, where all of the offspring have white flowers? Complete the table to show this. **(1 mark)**
   Total: 8 marks

4. This diagram shows a section through the eye.

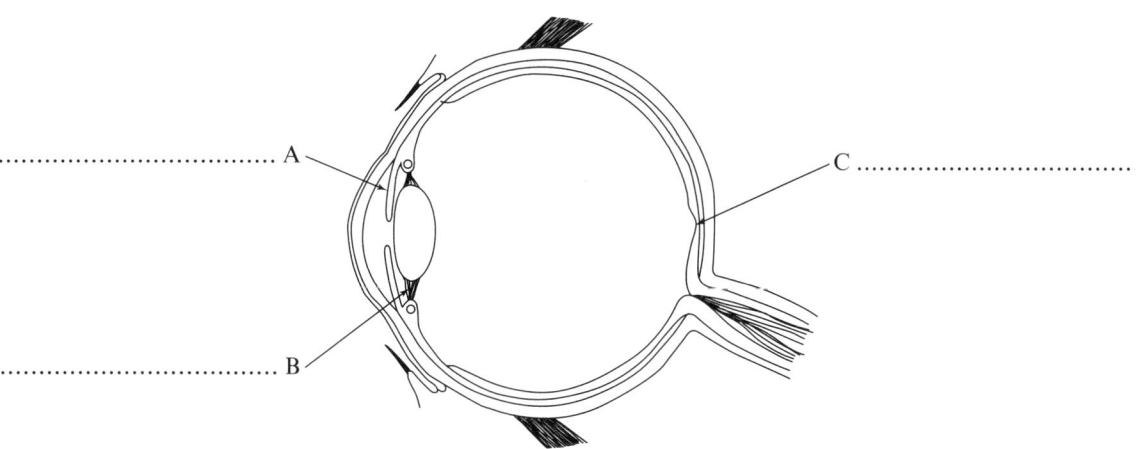

(a) Label the parts shown. **(3 marks)**

(b) Choose words from the box to complete this passage. Words may be used once, more than once, or not at all.

rods	muscle	optic	brain
choroid	lens	motor	cones
pupil	retina	cornea	short and fat
eye	contracted	relaxed	long and thin

When you look at a distant object, the lens is .... because the

ciliary muscles are .... A clear image is formed on the

...., where there are two types of sensory cells called

.... and .... Nerve impulses pass from these

sensory cells, along the .... nerve to the .... **(7 marks)**

(c) Diagram A shows the appearance of the pupil of the eye in normal light.

  (i) Complete diagram B to show how it would look in bright light. **(1 mark)**

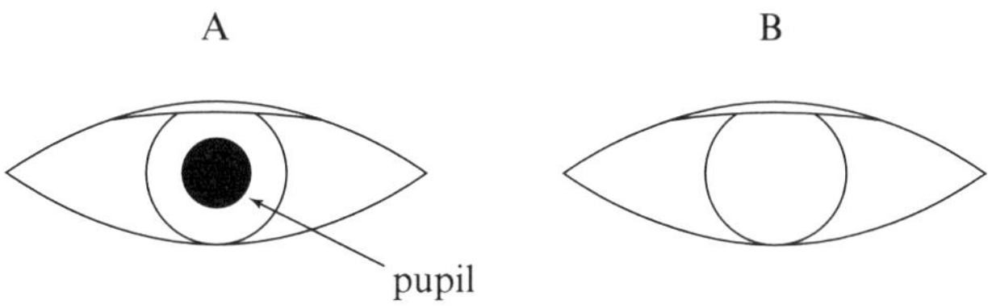

  (ii) This change in pupil size is an example of a reflex reaction.
  Put these statements about a reflex in the correct order.

  A Impulse passes through the motor neurone.

  B Receptor cells detect the stimulus.

  C Impulse passes through the sensory neurone.

  D Effector causes the response, e.g. muscle contracts.

  E Impulse passes through the relay neurone.

  (1 mark)

Turn over

(iii) When the pupil changes in size, what is the stimulus?

....

(1 mark)

(iv) Which muscle is the effector? (Be as precise as possible.)

....

(1 mark)
Total: 14 marks

5. Normal peppered moths are a pale, speckled colour. Occasionally, dark moths are born as a result of a mutation.

   (a) (i) Why does the colour of the moths affect their chance of survival?

   ....

   .... **(1 mark)**

   (ii) Which type of moth, pale or dark, would you expect to survive longest in an industrial area?

   ....

   .... **(1 mark)**

   (iii) Explain the reason for this.

   ....

   .... **(1 mark)**

   (b) A scientist carried out a survey where he trapped large numbers of peppered moths, and calculated the proportions of pale and dark moths in different areas of Britain. The map shows his results.

(i) What general trend can you see in these results?

....

(1 mark)

(ii) Cornwall and East Anglia are both non-industrial areas. Suggest a reason why the results are so different for these two areas.

....

....

....

(1 mark)

(c) In Ireland the pale moths have a selective advantage. Explain what this means.

....

....

....

(2 marks)

(d) (i) Which of these is an example of natural selection?

  A Pedigree dogs being developed by a breeding programme.

  B Tomatoes being genetically engineered to ripen earlier.

  C Rats becoming resistant to Warfarin (rat poison).

  D Wheat being improved by selective breeding.

  E Bacteria producing human insulin.

  Answer .... **(1 mark)**

(ii) Give a reason for your choice.

....

....

....

(1 mark)
Total: 9 marks

Turn over

6. A student set up an experiment to investigate how fast leaf discs decay. She cut 2 cm discs from a leaf using a cork borer, soaked them in disinfectant to sterilise them, weighed them, then placed 40 into each of three types of bags.

Bag A – made of nylon mesh, with a mesh size of 5 mm

Bag B – made of nylon mesh, with a mesh size of 0.5 mm

Bag C – made of clear polythene

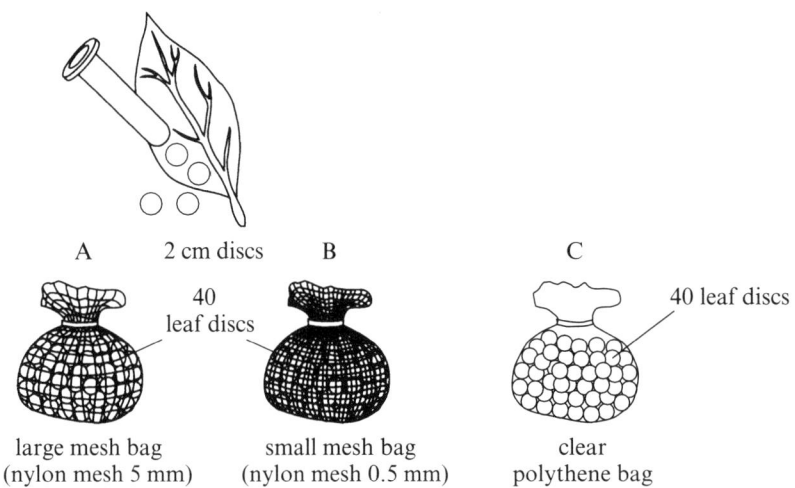

She buried the bags in the garden for 10 weeks, then dug them up, weighed the leaf samples and calculated the percentage change in mass.

(a) (i) Which of the bags would you expect to have the greatest change in mass?

....
(1 mark)

(ii) Explain why ....

....
(1 mark)

(b) (i) One of the bags had no change in mass at all, i.e. decay had not occurred. Which bag was this? .... **(1 mark)**

(ii) Explain why ....

....

....
(1 mark)

(c) Name two types of organism which cause decay.

.... and .... **(2 marks)**
Total: 6 marks

7. The diagram shows a kidney tubule (nephron) and the blood vessel next to it.

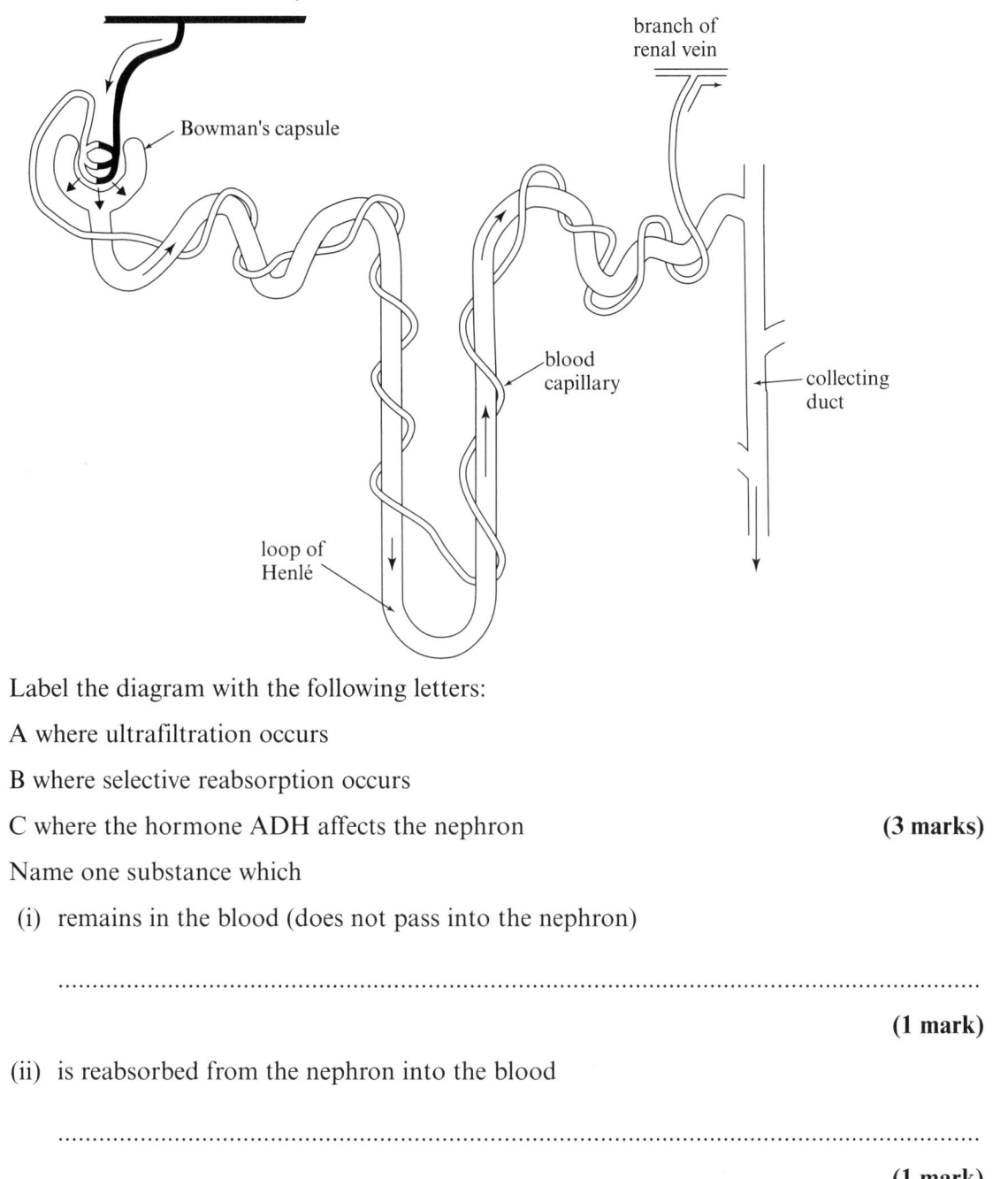

(a) Label the diagram with the following letters:

A where ultrafiltration occurs

B where selective reabsorption occurs

C where the hormone ADH affects the nephron **(3 marks)**

(b) Name one substance which

(i) remains in the blood (does not pass into the nephron)

....

(1 mark)

(ii) is reabsorbed from the nephron into the blood

....

(1 mark)

(iii) is not reabsorbed from the nephron at all

....

(1 mark)

(c) Select the correct alternatives, by underlining them, in this passage about ADH.

ADH is produced when a person has drunk a lot/a person has exercised a lot/a person is tired. It increases/does not affect/decreases the permeability of the nephron to water, so more/less/dilute urine is produced. **(3 marks)**

Total: 9 marks

Turn over

8. The diagram shows a food web for a wood.

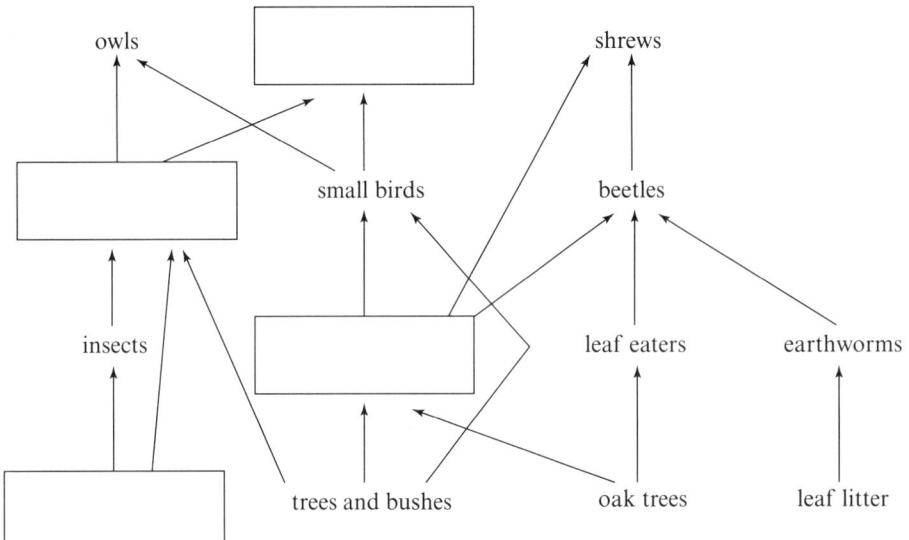

(a) Use the information given in the table to fill in the boxes and complete the food web.
(4 marks)

Organism	What it eats
beetles	moths, earthworms, leaf eaters
shrews	beetles, moths
voles	insects, herbs, trees and bushes
weasels	voles, small birds
earthworms	leaf litter
owls	voles, small birds
leaf eaters	oak trees
insects	herbs
small birds	moths, trees and bushes
moths	trees and bushes, oak trees

(b) Choose the words from the box which best describe each of the following organisms.

primary consumer	omnivore	producer
carnivore	secondary consumer	top carnivore
tertiary consumer	herbivore	

(i) oak tree ....

(ii) moth .... and ....

(iii) shrew .... and ....

(iv) vole .... (4 marks)

(c) Consider the food chain shown here.

oak trees ⟶ leaf eaters ⟶ beetles ⟶ shrews

(i) Which pyramid of numbers represents this food chain? **(1 mark)**

A   C

B   D

(ii) Sketch a pyramid of biomass for this food chain. **(1 mark)**

(iii) Explain why it is a different shape from the pyramid of numbers in part (c) (i).

....

....
(1 mark)

(d) This flow chart represents the energy flow through the food chain in part (c).

| 500 kJ | →90% energy loss→ | | →90% energy loss→ | 5 kJ | →90% energy loss→ | 0.5 kJ |

oak tree   leaf eaters   beetles   shrews

(i) Calculate the energy which is passed on to the leaf eaters from the oak trees.

Answer .... **(1 mark)**

(ii) State one process which results in a loss of energy between one step and the next.

....
(1 mark)
Total: 13 marks

9. (a) The diagram shows the cells and cell fragments found in blood. Three of these help to defend the body from disease.

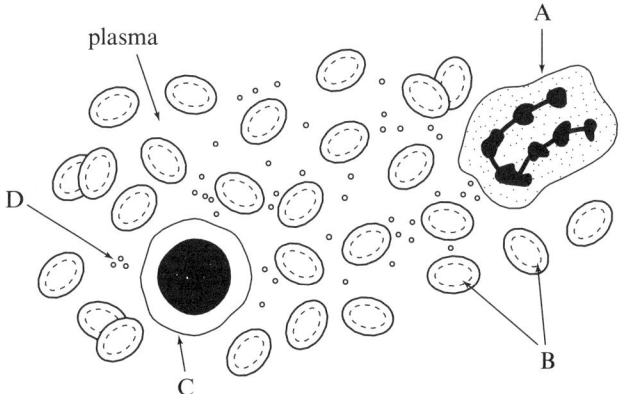

Turn over

Complete the table to show which cells or cell fragments are involved in defence against disease, and how they do this. **(6 marks)**

Letter	Name of cell or cell fragment	How it defends the body from disease

(b) Which type of cell or cell fragment is activated by immunisation (vaccination)?

....

(1 mark)

(c) The graph shows what happens the first time the body is exposed to an antigen.

(i) Extend the line to show what happens the next time it is exposed to the same antigen **(1 mark)**

(ii) Use this information to explain how immunisation prevents disease.

....

....

....

....

....

(4 marks)
Total: 12 marks

10. The diagram shows some of the steps in the nitrogen cycle.

    (a) (i) Complete the box to show the form in which plants take up nitrogen
         (1 mark)

    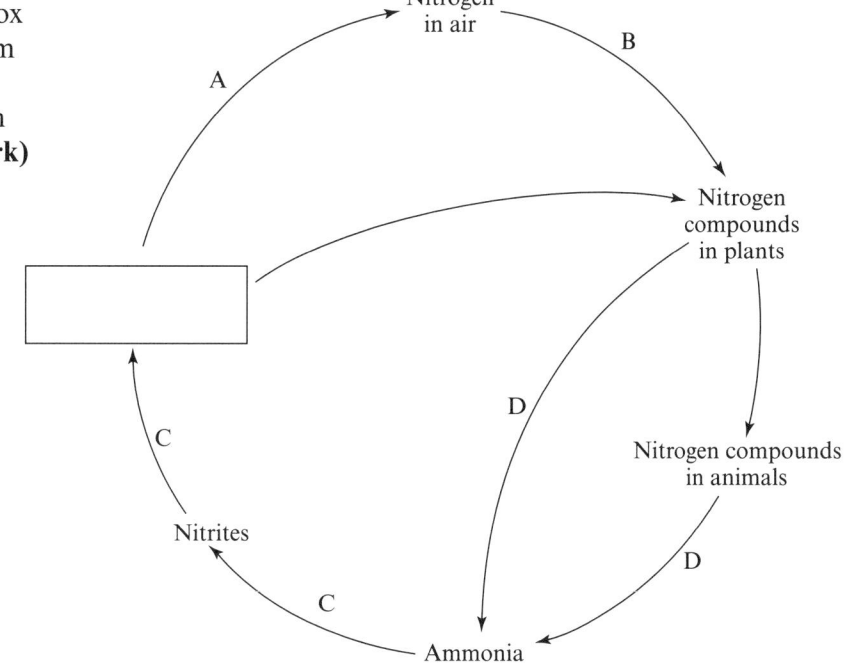

    (ii) How do plants use nitrogen?

    ....

    (1 mark)

    (b) (i) What types of bacteria are involved in the following steps?

        A ....

        B ....

        C ....

        D ....

    (4 marks)

    (ii) Where do the bacteria which carry out step B live?

    ....

    (1 mark)
    Total: 7 marks

Longman Examination Board

General Certificate of Secondary Education
Biology
Paper 3

Time: 90 minutes

Instructions

- Answer all questions in the spaces provided in this exam paper.
- Show all stages in any calculations, and state the units. You may use a calculator if you wish.
- Include diagrams in your answers where these are helpful.

Information for candidates

- The marks for various parts of questions are shown in brackets, e.g. (1 mark).
- This exam paper has 10 questions.
- You are allowed 90 minutes for this paper.
- The maximum mark for this paper is 100.

Number	Mark
1.	
2.	
3.	
4.	
5.	
6.	
7.	
8.	
9.	
10.	

---

1. (a) (i) Put ticks in the appropriate boxes in the table below to show the features of root hair cells and egg cells (ova). **(2 marks)**

	Nucleus	Cell wall	Sap vacuole	Genes
Root hair cell				
Egg cell (ovum)				

   (ii) State one part of the cell not named in the table, which is found in both types of cells.

   ....

   (1 mark)

   (iii) Which type of cell division occurs to form

   root hair cells ....

   egg cells ....

   (2 marks)

Leave margin blank

(b) The diagrams show two different types of cells, A and B.
Name each type of cell, state its function, and one way it is adapted for its function.

A   B

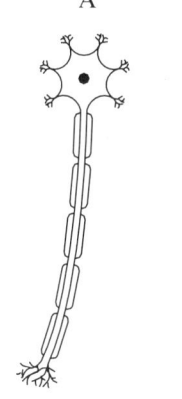 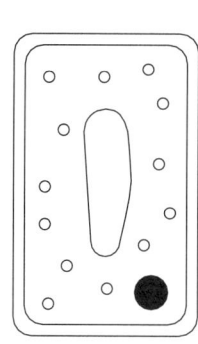

Name of A .... **(1 mark)**

Function .... **(1 mark)**

How it is adapted ....

.... **(1 mark)**

Name of B .... **(1 mark)**

Function .... **(1 mark)**

How it is adapted ....

.... **(1 mark)**

Total: 11 marks

2. The diagram shows a potometer. This apparatus is used to measure transpiration rate in plants.

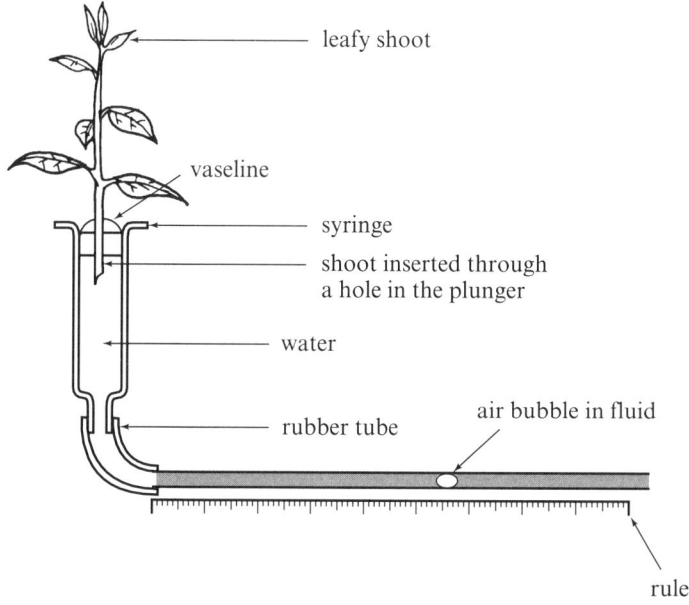

(a) In which direction does the bubble move?

....

(1 mark)

Turn over

(b) It is possible to modify the apparatus to change the conditions the shoot is exposed to, e.g. by altering the amount of light; by putting a fan close to the plant; by enclosing the shoot in a clear polythene bag.

(i) Use the figures below to complete the table. **(1 mark)**

       0.3   2.6   7.8

	Conditions	Distance travelled by bubble in 5 minutes (cm)
A	Light, no fan, shoot not in bag	5.7
B	Light, fan close to shoot, shoot not in bag	
C	Light, no fan, shoot enclosed in clear bag	
D	Dark, no fan, shoot not in bag	

(ii) Suggest an explanation for each of the results, compared to A.

B ....

....

C ....

....

D ....

....

(3 marks)

(iii) In experiment A, how would the rate of transpiration change if the temperature was 5 °C higher?

....

(1 mark)

(c) Give two reasons why transpiration is important to plants.

....

....

(2 marks)
Total: 8 marks

3. The diagram shows the human digestive system.

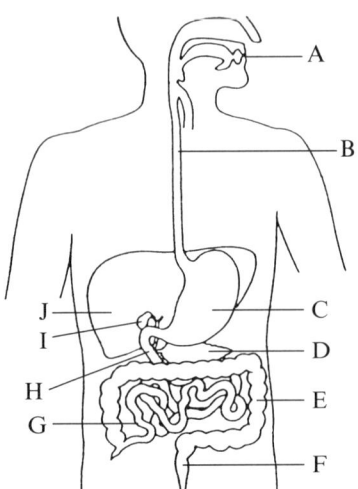

(a) (i) Which letter represents the part where bile is produced? .... **(1 mark)**

(ii) What does bile do?

....

(1 mark)

(b) (i) Which letter represents the part which has villi? .... **(1 mark)**

(ii) What do villi do?

....

(1 mark)

(c) (i) Which letter represents the part where acid is produced? .... **(1 mark)**

(ii) Give one function of this acid.

....

....

(1 mark)

(d) (i) Enzymes are produced in several parts of the digestive system. Which letter from the diagram represents one of the parts where protease is produced?

.... **(1 mark)**

(ii) Complete the table about digestive enzymes. **(6 marks)**

Name of enzyme	Substance it digests	Products which are formed
protease		
	starch	
		fatty acids and glycerol

Total: 13 marks

4. Haemophilia is a sex-linked condition, caused by a recessive allele. People who suffer from the disease have blood which will not clot properly.
Use the symbols **H** for the allele for normal blood clotting, and **h** for the allele for haemophilia in this question.

(a) One possible genotype for a woman is $X^H X^H$.
Write down all other possible genotypes for women and men.

Women ....

Men .... **(2 marks)**

(b) This pedigree (family tree) shows how haemophilia has been inherited in one family.

Key
- haemophiliac male
- normal male
- haemophiliac woman
- normal woman
- carrier woman

Mr Jones — Mrs Jones
Children: Sara, David, Lucy, Kate

(i) What are the genotypes of Mr and Mrs Jones?

Mr Jones .... Mrs Jones .... **(2 marks)**

(ii) Explain how you arrived at your answer.

....
....
....
....

(3 marks)

(iii) What is the probability that Kate suffers from haemophilia?

....

(1 mark)

(iv) Explain how you arrived at your answer.

....
....
....

(2 marks)
Total: 10 marks

5. The diagram below shows the carbon cycle.

Carbon dioxide in air — A, B (Plants), A (Animals), C (Humus), Fossil fuels

(a) (i) Name the processes labelled A, B and C.

A ....

B ....

C .... **(3 marks)**

(ii) Which of these steps involves bacteria? .... **(1 mark)**

(iii) Name the type of bacteria involved.

....

(1 mark)

(b) (i) Which important environmental change is associated with increased levels of carbon dioxide in the air?

....

(1 mark)

(ii) Suggest one cause of increased carbon dioxide.

....

(1 mark)

(c) (i) If fuels are incompletely burned, a carbon compound not named in the table is formed. What is it?

....

(1 mark)

(ii) What problems does it cause if it is inhaled by humans?

....

....

(2 marks)
Total: 10 marks

6. (a) Underline the phrase from the list which **best** describes what hormones are.

chemicals made by glands

a message which helps to co-ordinate body activities

a chemical which lowers the blood sugar level

a chemical which has an effect on a target organ

a chemical which travels in the blood **(1 mark)**

Turn over

(b) Complete the table about hormones. **(5 marks)**

Name of hormone	Where it is produced	When it is produced	Effect of hormone
insulin	pancreas	after a meal	lowers blood sugar level
	pituitary gland		reduces amount of urine produced
			raises heart rate and breathing rate

Total: 6 marks

7. Humus is decaying organic matter that is found in soil, e.g. dead leaves, plant roots, animal faeces, etc. Different samples of soil contain different amounts of humus. As the humus decays (is broken down by decomposers), carbon dioxide is released.
Gemma wanted to find out which of three soil samples contained the most humus, so she set up an investigation, using the following soils.

A–soil from a wood

B–soil from a farmers field, where crops had just been harvested

C–soil from waste ground, where buildings had just been demolished

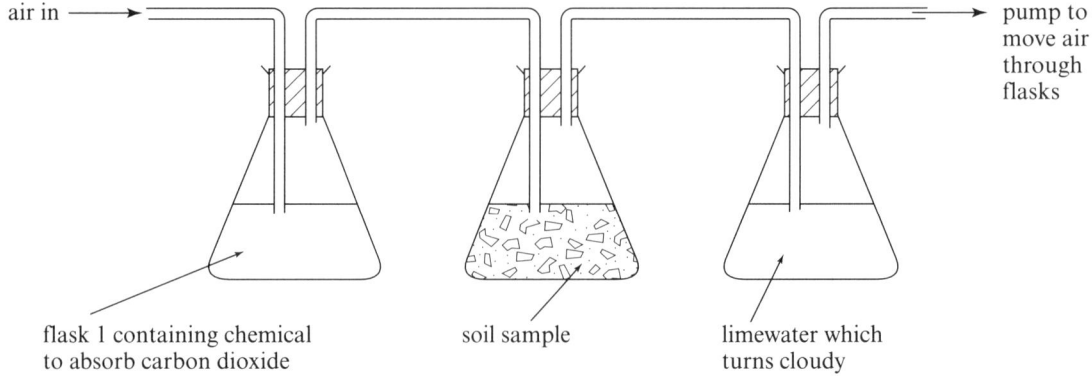

(a) (i) Which chemical could you put in flask 1 to absorb carbon dioxide?

....

(1 mark)

(ii) Would a sample containing a lot of humus turn the limewater cloudy quickly or slowly?

....

(1 mark)

She recorded the time taken for the limewater to turn cloudy, then repeated the experiment with each soil sample.

(b) State three things she must do to make sure it is a fair test.

....

....

....

(3 marks)

(c) (i) How could she keep the temperature constant in this experiment?

....

(1 mark)

(ii) How would the results be different if the temperature was higher?

....

(1 mark)

(d) (i) Which soil sample would you expect to contain the most humus? .... **(1 mark)**

(ii) Give a reason for your choice.

....

....

(1 mark)

(e) What else, apart from decaying humus, could be releasing carbon dioxide?

....

(1 mark)

(f) Suggest two ways she could improve her experiment.

....

....

(2 marks)
Total: 12 marks

8. (a) The diagram shows part of a DNA molecule. The letters A, T, C and G represent the four bases. Only letters A and C are shown in the diagram.

(i) What are A and C abbreviations for?

A.. C.. **(2 marks)**

(ii) Complete the diagram by writing the correct letters in the empty boxes. **(1 mark)**

Turn over

(iii) What term is used to describe the shape of the DNA molecule?

....

(1 mark)

(b) The sequence of the bases in DNA carries information about the order of amino acids needed to make a particular protein. This is called the genetic code.

(i) What is the name for a section of DNA which codes for one protein?

....

(1 mark)

The table shows the DNA bases needed to code for particular amino acids.

DNA sequence	Amino acid	DNA sequence	Amino acid
AAA	phenylalanine	TTT	lysine
CCC	glycine	GGG	proline
CTG	aspartic acid	CAT	valine
GTG	histidine	TCA	serine
TCC	arginine	ACC	tryptophan
TGA	threonine	CTT	glutamic acid

(ii) If the DNA sequence was TGACATGTCGGG, what are the first two amino acids coded for in this sequence?

....

(1 mark)

(iii) If an error is made when the DNA copies itself, the genetic code will be altered. What is an error like this called?

....

(1 mark)

(iv) The error results in a changed sequence of bases as follows:

original sequence TGACATGTCGGG

changed sequence TGACTTGTCGGG

What are the first two amino acids in this sequence now?

....

(1 mark)

(c) A condition called sickle-cell anaemia is caused by a copying error like the one described above.
Sickle-cell anaemia is a genetic disease where the red blood cells are the wrong shape.

(i) What term is used to describe the normal shape of a red blood cell?

....

(1 mark)

(ii) Suggest one disadvantage of having red blood cells that are sickled.

....

(1 mark)
Total: 10 marks

9. This graph gives information about the number of kidney transplants occurring in Britain, and the number of people waiting for transplants.

(a) (i) How many transplants took place in 1984?

....

(1 mark)

(ii) How many people needed a transplant but could not have one in 1995?

....

(1 mark)

Turn over

(b) Suggest two possible reasons why the number of people on the waiting list has risen, even though the number of transplants has not decreased.

....

....

(2 marks)

(c) Explain as fully as you can why it is important for the kidney donor and the recipient to be carefully matched.

....

....

....

....

(4 marks)

(d) If a transplant is not available, a person with kidney failure may be treated with dialysis. The process used is shown in the diagram below.

(i) Why is the tube coiled?

....

....

(1 mark)

(ii) Name three substances you would expect to pass from the blood into the dialysis fluid.

....

(3 marks)

(iii) Why should the dialysis fluid contain glucose at the same concentration as the glucose in blood?

....

....

(2 marks)
Total: 14 marks

Leave margin blank

10. Scientists have carried out genetic engineering to develop bacteria which can make human insulin.

(a) (i) What effect does insulin have in the body?

    ....
    (1 mark)

(ii) If a person cannot make their own insulin, what disease do they have?

    ....
    (1 mark)

(b) The following steps in the production of insulin by bacteria are in the wrong order, write the letter in the correct order in the box below.

   A. Collect insulin and purify it

   B. Transfer the gene into a vector, e.g. plasmid

   C. Identify the gene for insulin in humans

   D. Grow large numbers of bacteria in a fermenter

   E. Cut out the gene using enzymes

   F. Transfer the vector containing the gene into bacteria

   | | | | | | |

   (1 mark)

(c) (i) Some bacteria can use nitrogen gas to make proteins. What are these bacteria called?

    ....
    (1 mark)

(ii) Why would it be an advantage to humans if the gene which allows them to do this could be transferred to crop plants, e.g. wheat?

    ....

    ....

    (2 marks)
    Total: 6 marks

Solutions to practice exam papers

Marking instructions

When you mark your answers, follow these simple rules:

- Each * represents 1 mark.
- If an answer is marked ‡ it means that there are several alternative answers. The maximum mark for that part of the question is written beside it.
- If part of an answer is written in brackets, it is **not** needed to achieve the mark.
- Make sure the answer is correct before you award yourself the mark – do not be too generous about answers which are 'nearly right'. If you are not sure, ask your teacher or another responsible person.

Solutions to Paper 1

1. (a) The missing words are:
   nucleus*; DNA*; 46*; mitosis*; meiosis*; mitosis*; diploid/chromosome*; haploid*; gametes/eggs/sperm*   **9 marks**

   (b) (i) C, B, A, E, D*   **1 mark**   (ii) mitosis*   **1 mark**

   (iii) There are two daughter cells* (in meiosis there would be four).‡
   The daughter cells have the same number of chromosomes as the original cell *
   (in meiosis they would have half the original number).‡   **1 mark**

   Total: 12 marks

2. (a) (i) oxygen is produced in photosynthesis*   **1 mark**

   (ii) carbon dioxide is produced in respiration*   **1 mark**

   > **TIP**
   > This question is testing your understanding of the relationship between photosynthesis and respiration. Remember **all** organisms carry out respiration **all the time**, but only plants photosynthesise and they need light to do it.

   (b) **10 marks**

Tube	Colour of bicarbonate indicator after 4 hours	Explanation
A	purple*	Pondweed is photosynthesising, so it is using up carbon dioxide*
B	yellow*	Pond snails are respiring, so they are producing carbon dioxide*
C	red*	Pondweed is photosynthesising, and using carbon dioxide, snails are respiring, so there is a **balance** i.e. no change in colour*
D	very yellow*	Pondweed cannot photosynthesise in the dark. Both pondweed and pond snails are respiring, so both are producing carbon dioxide*
E	red*	There are no living organisms in the tube to affect carbon dioxide levels, so the colour does not change. This is a control tube*

> **TIP**
> Students often lose marks because they forget that plants respire!

Total: 12 marks

3. (a) (i) The allele causing the disease is recessive*. **1 mark**
 Individuals 1 and 2 do not have the disease but two of their children do*. **1 mark**

    (ii) This disease is not sex-linked*. **1 mark**
 It seems to affect males and females equally often* (if it was sex-linked, males would be more often affected than females). **1 mark**

   (b) Dd* and Dd* **2 marks**

   (c) This disease is most like cystic fibrosis*. **1 mark**
 (Haemophilia is sex-linked, and Huntington's disease is caused by a dominant allele.)

Total: 7 marks

> **TIP**
> You should be familiar with how to analyse a pedigree (family tree). Look for patterns in the way the disease is passed on, and whether males and females are equally likely to be sufferers. You can identify carriers if they do not have the disease themselves, but their children do.

4. (a) sugar/maltose/glucose is formed* **1 mark**

   (b) (i) black* **1 mark**

    (ii) A – the amylase in the seed is spreading through the jelly and digesting the starch* **1 mark**

     B – the amylase has been denatured/destroyed by the heat* **1 mark**

     C – the amylase has been denatured/destroyed by the acid* **1 mark**

     D – the amylase cannot escape from the uncut seed (the seedcoat is impermeable to it)* **1 mark**

    (iii) There would be a clear zone around the seed*.
 The zone would be smaller than the one in the diagram for seed A (because maize contains less amylase)*. **2 marks**

Total: 8 marks

5. (a)

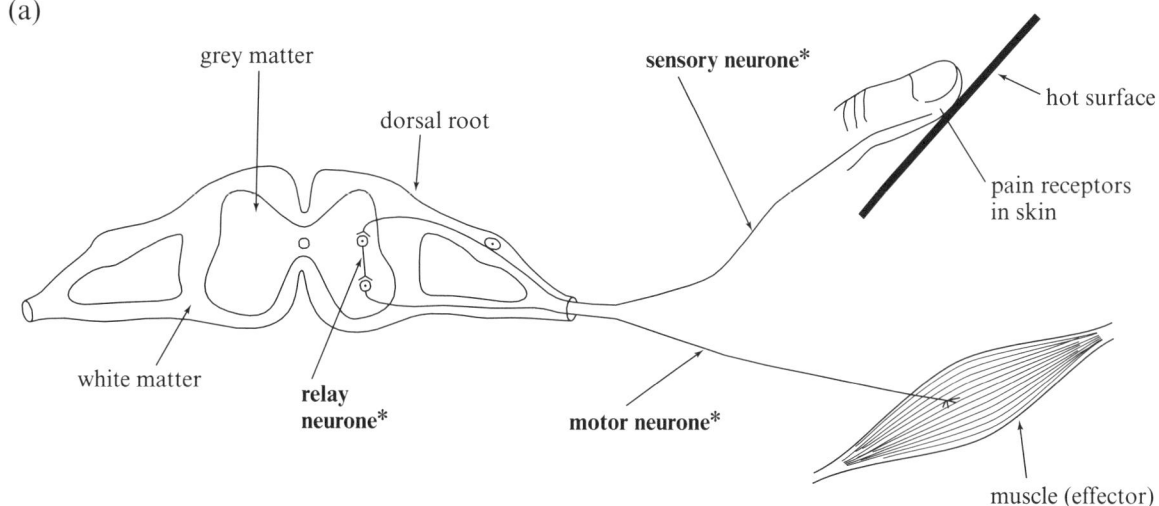

Labels: grey matter, dorsal root, **sensory neurone***, hot surface, pain receptors in skin, white matter, **relay neurone***, **motor neurone***, muscle (effector)

3 marks

(b) a synapse* **1 mark**

(c)

Name of reflex	Stimulus	Response
withdrawal reflex	pain, e.g. hot object touches skin	muscle contracts to move the body away from the stimulus
pupil reflex*	**bright light***	pupil decreases in size
choke reflex*	food or liquid in the trachea	**cough to remove food/liquid from trachea***

4 marks

(d) (i) There are several possible answers here,

e.g. A reflex action involves three neurones, a voluntary action involves more than this*. ‡

A reflex action occurs much more quickly than a voluntary action. ‡

A reflex action is unlearned/automatic, a voluntary action is not. ‡

A reflex action does not involve the brain, but a voluntary action does. ‡   **1 mark**

> **TIP**
> Make sure that you include a statement about both a reflex and a voluntary action to gain the two marks.

Total: 9 marks

6. (a) Modern wheat has a shorter stem*, so it is less likely to be blown over/damaged by strong winds or bad weather* (this makes it easier to harvest). ‡
Modern wheat has a longer ear*, so that each plant produces more grain/has a higher yield*. ‡
Modern wheat has more grains*, so that the plants have a higher yield/provide more food*. ‡   **2 marks**

(b) Any one difference and its benefit, from:

disease resistant*, so that crops will have a better chance of survival* ‡

higher proportion of protein/carbohydrate in the grain*, so that the food produced is more nutritious* ‡

grows at higher temperatures*, so that it is suitable for tropical countries* ‡   **2 marks**

> **TIP**
> You are not expected to know the answer to part (b), but any sensible suggestion would gain you marks.

(c) If the plant was cloned, the offspring would be identical*, so they would all be equally useful to humans*.‡ Plants formed by sexual reproduction are not identical to their parents*, so useful features could be lost*.‡ **2 marks**

Total: 6 marks

7. (a) (i) E* (ii) A or B* (ii) D* and G*   **4 marks**

(b) (i) capillary* **1 mark**

(ii) A – carbon dioxide* B – oxygen* **2 marks**

(iii) respiration produces gas A* **1 mark**

(iv) the gases diffuse* **1 mark**

(c) (i) balloons – lungs*; rubber sheet – diaphragm*; bell jar – rib-cage/chest wall/thorax
3 marks

(ii) the balloons will decrease in size/deflate* **1 mark**

(iii) When the sheet is pushed up: the volume in the bell jar decreases*; so the pressure inside the bell jar increases*; so air is forced out of the balloons*. **3 marks**

> **TIP**
> Make sure you are familiar with this model – it is often used to test your understanding of the processes involved in ventilation. It depends on changes in **volume** and **pressure** inside the bell jars.

Total: 16 marks

8. (a) (i) ovulation = day 14*   (ii) menstruation starts on day 1* **2 marks**

   (b) A = oestrogen*   B = progesterone* **2 marks**

   (c) (i) B is produced in large amounts in pregnancy* (ii) The placenta secretes it* **2 marks**

   (d) Any **one** from:

   A – (umbilical cord); carries antibodies from the mother to the foetus. These protect it from disease*. ‡

   E – (amniotic fluid); cushions the foetus from bumps as the mother moves around*. ‡

   F – (plug of mucus); blocks the cervix to stop bacteria entering the uterus*. ‡ **1 mark**

Total: 7 marks

> **TIP**
> There are several correct alternatives that you could choose for part (d). The key to gaining marks is describing how the foetus is protected.

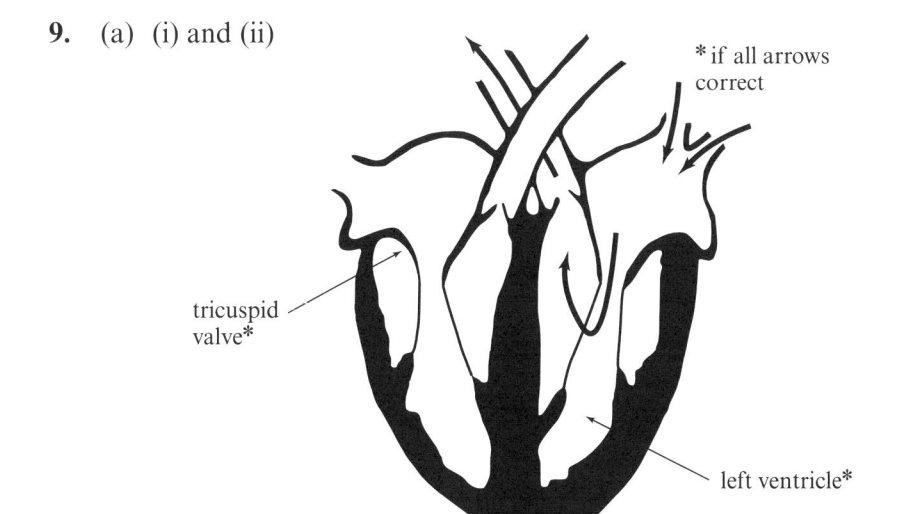

9. (a) (i) and (ii)

*if all arrows correct

tricuspid valve*

left ventricle*

3 marks.

> **TIP**
> If you put any arrows on the right side of the heart (deoxygenated blood) you would not get any marks for part (ii).

(b) (i) C (pulmonary artery)* (ii) B (aorta)* **2 marks**

(c) (i) X is muscle* (cardiac muscle) **1 mark**

   (ii) Y can pump harder/contract more strongly, to force blood further/to push blood around the body*; X is not pushing the blood so far/is pumping blood to the lungs* **2 marks**

(d) (i) Q is cholesterol/fatty material* **1 mark**

   (ii) the person could have angina/a heart attack/heart muscle would die* **1 mark**

   (iii) Factors linked to heart disease include: being overweight*; eating a high fat diet*; lack of exercise*; smoking*; stress*. Any two of these for 2 marks. **2 marks**

   Total: 12 marks

10. (a) (i) The numbers of bacteria rise as there is more sewage for them to feed on*; they are decomposers/they break down the sewage*; the numbers fall as all of the sewage is broken down/their food supply is reduced.* **3 marks**

   (ii) The dissolved oxygen level falls because bacteria use oxygen*; the level rises again when the number of bacteria falls/oxygen is mixed with the water, e.g. in waterfalls or weirs.* **2 marks**

   (iii) The number of fish decreases because they do not have enough oxygen to survive*; where more oxygen is available (downstream), the number increases.* **2 marks**

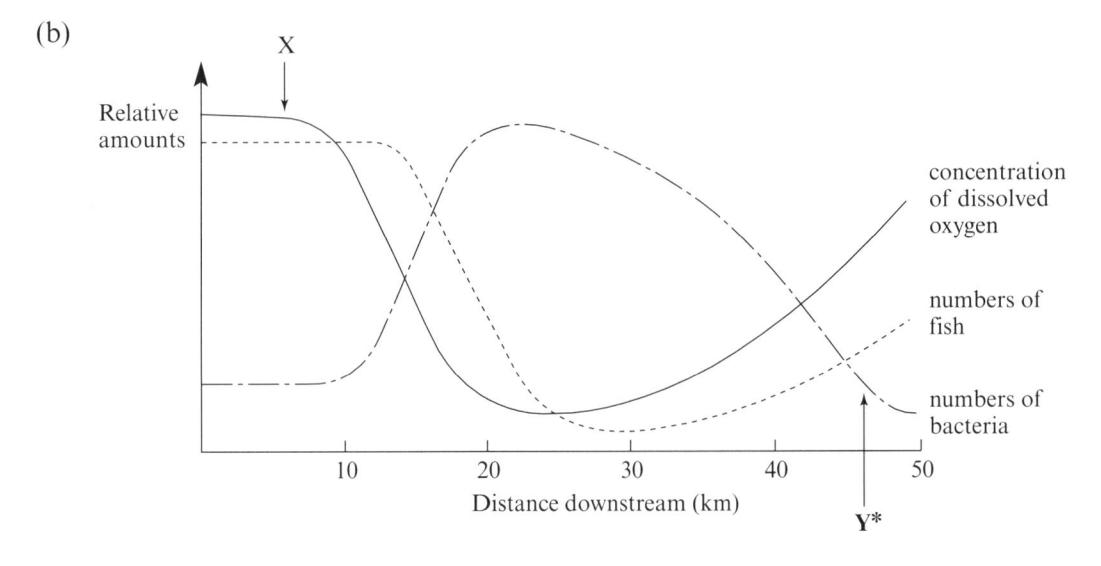

(b) [Graph showing Relative amounts vs Distance downstream (km), with curves for concentration of dissolved oxygen, numbers of fish, and numbers of bacteria. X labelled at top of one curve, Y* labelled near 45 km.] **1 mark**

TIP
Make sure that you mark this clearly: use a label line, not a large letter written on the diagram.

(c) (i) The numbers of algae will increase*. **1 mark**

   (ii) When the algae die, the amount of oxygen in the water decreases (as decay occurs)*; this is eutrophication*. **2 marks**

   Total: 11 marks

Solutions to Paper 2

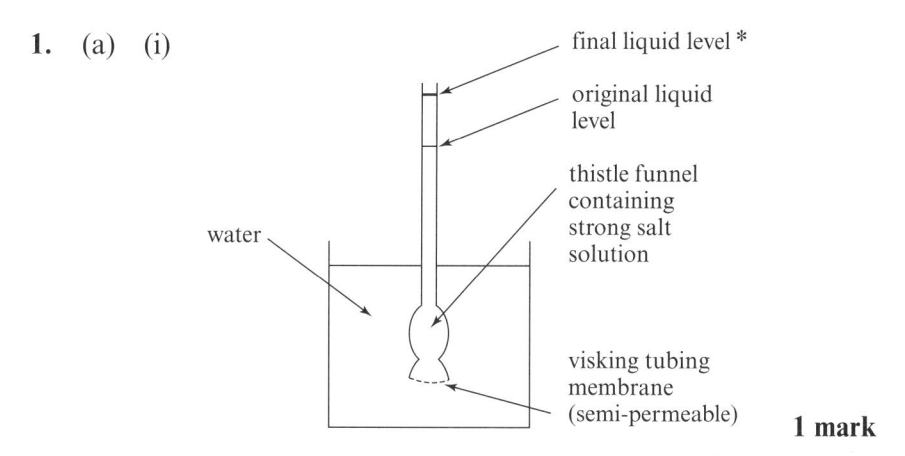

1. (a) (i)

Diagram: thistle funnel containing strong salt solution inverted in a beaker of water, with visking tubing membrane (semi-permeable) at the bulb; arrows indicate final liquid level (*) and original liquid level in the funnel stem. **1 mark**

  (ii) Water moved into the funnel* by osmosis* because there was a higher concentration of water molecules in the beaker than the funnel*‡. **2 marks**

 (b) (i) cell A*   (ii) the cell is turgid*   (iii) the cell membrane (both are semi-permeable)*.
3 marks
Total: 6 marks

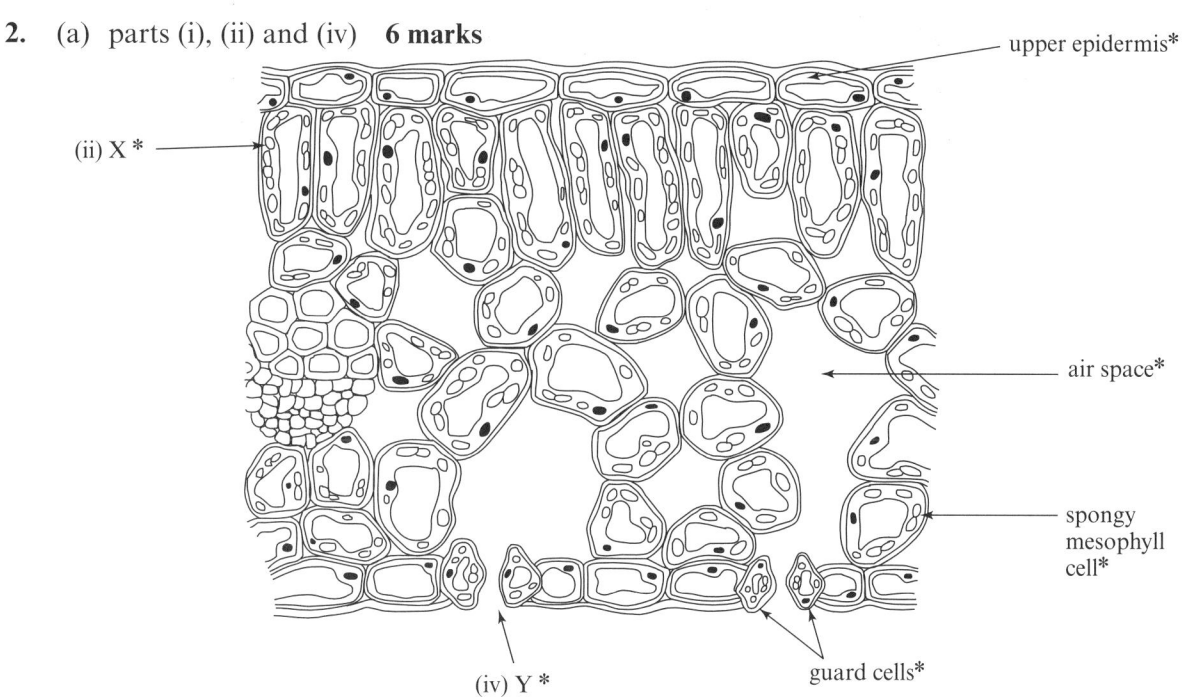

2. (a) parts (i), (ii) and (iv) **6 marks**

Diagram of leaf cross-section labelled: upper epidermis, (ii) X* (palisade layer), air space*, spongy mesophyll cell*, guard cells*, (iv) Y* (stoma).*

  (iii) oxygen is produced in photosynthesis*   **1 mark**

(b) (i) *for labelling the bars *for drawing them accurately *for adding a suitable scale to the y-axis   **3 marks**

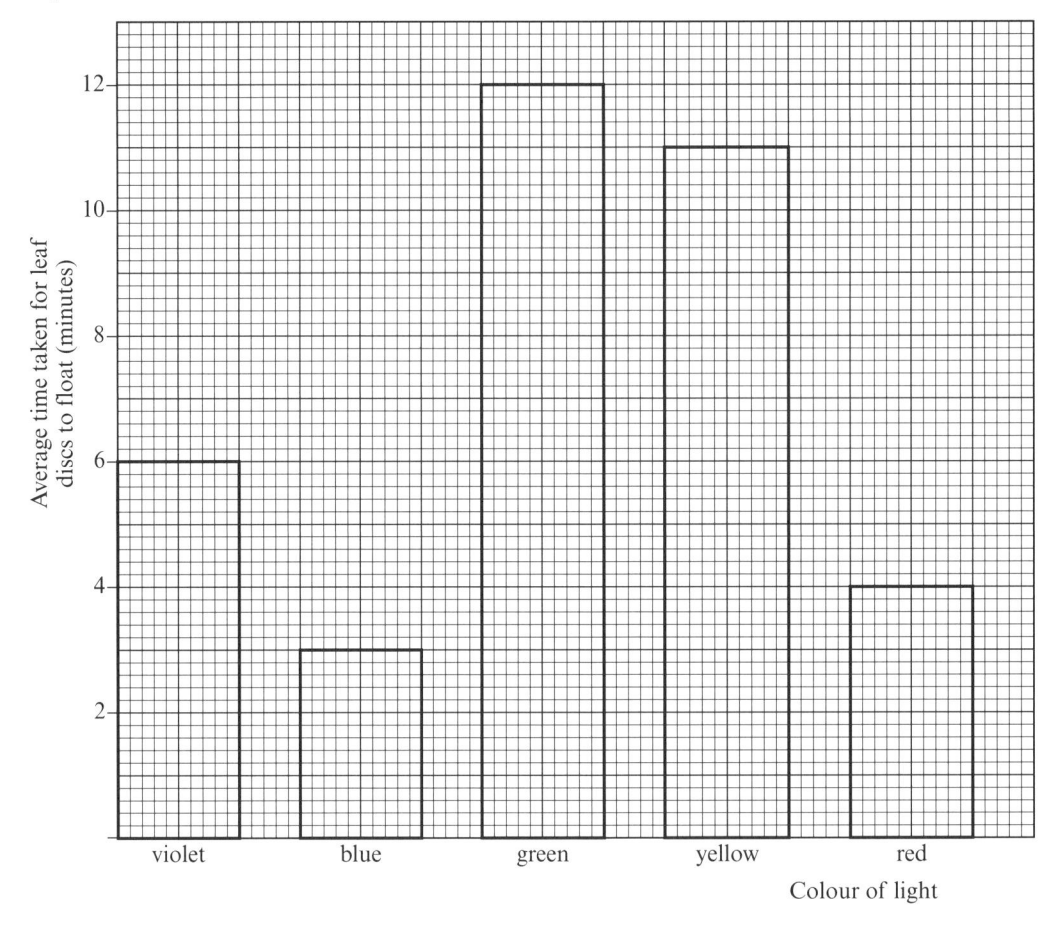

[Bar chart: y-axis "Average time taken for leaf discs to float (minutes)" from 0 to 12; x-axis "Colour of light" with bars — violet: 6, blue: 3, green: 12, yellow: 11, red: 4]

> **TIP**
> Make sure that you choose a suitable scale, and label your bars clearly to get full marks.

(ii) blue light*   **1 mark**

> **TIP**
> Remember, a large bar means it took a long time for the leaf discs to float, so photosynthesis was occurring slowly. If you got this answer wrong you probably rushed into your answer, without reading the information you were given about the experiment. Go back and read it carefully now.

(iii) It releases carbon dioxide when it dissolves*; this increases the rate of photosynthesis*.   **2 marks**

(iv) So that an average could be calculated/to provide more reliable results/to reduce the chance of error*.   **1 mark**

(v) Any two of:

make sure that the tubes all had equal amounts of light/light of the same intensity*‡

add equal amounts of sodium hydrogen carbonate to each tube*‡

make sure that all the leaf discs were the same size*‡

all leaf discs should come from the same type of leaf*‡

the temperature should be the same in each tube*‡   **2 marks**

Total: 16 marks

3. (a) (i) homozygous* (ii) haploid/gamete/egg/sperm* (iii) dominant* (iv) sex-linked*
4 marks

(b) parts (i) and (ii) **4 marks**

		Phenotypes of offspring	
Cross	Genotypes of parents	Plants with purple flowers	Plants with white flowers
A	FF × FF	✓	*
B	Ff × ff	✓	✓ *
C	Ff × Ff	✓	✓ *
D	ff × ff*		✓

Total: 8 marks

4. (a) A = iris* B = suspensory ligaments* C = yellow spot* **3 marks**

(b) The missing words are: long and thin*; relaxed*; retina*; rods*; cones*; optic*; brain*.
7 marks

(c) (i) *mark given for showing the pupil much smaller than in diagram A **1 mark**

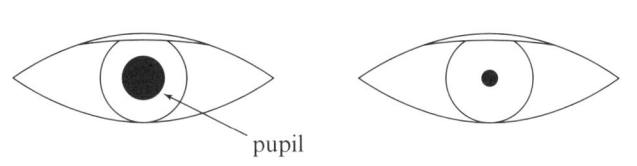

(ii) B, C, E, A, D* (iii) the stimulus is light* (iv) the radial muscles of the iris are the effector* **3 marks**

TIP
This question requires a lot of knowledge about the eye, and about the processes involved in a reflex. You need to revise very thoroughly to get high marks.

Total: 14 marks

5. (a) (i) If a moth is well camouflaged it is less likely to be eaten*. **1 mark**

(ii) dark moths* (iii) they are better camouflaged*‡/they are less likely to be eaten*‡/pollution blackens tree trunks where they rest*.‡ **2 marks**

(b) (i) There are more dark moths in cities/industrial areas*.‡ Rural areas have more light moths*.‡ **1 mark**

(ii) In East Anglia, prevailing winds are carrying pollution from industrial areas.* **1 mark**

(c) The pale moths are better suited/better adapted to their surroundings*; they are more likely to survive and breed*. **2 marks**

(d) (i) C* **1 mark**

(ii) Humans have not been involved directly in this process*.‡ The resistant rats were formed as a result of mutation, not deliberately developed*.‡ **1 mark**

Total: 9 marks

6. (a) (i) Bag A* **1 mark**

   (ii) The mesh size is large enough to allow small animals, e.g. beetles, worms, into the bag to eat the leaves*. **1 mark**

(b) (i) Bag C* **1 mark**

   (ii) The leaf discs were sterilised so that they did not contain any decomposers; the polythene bag did not allow decomposers in the soil to reach the leaf discs*. **1 mark**

(c) bacteria* and fungi* **2 marks**

Total: 6 marks

> **TIP**
> Questions on experiments involving decay are surprisingly common. The key to this question is the mesh size: a large mesh size allows bigger organisms to get into the bag, so the leaves in this bag will be broken down faster.

7. (a)

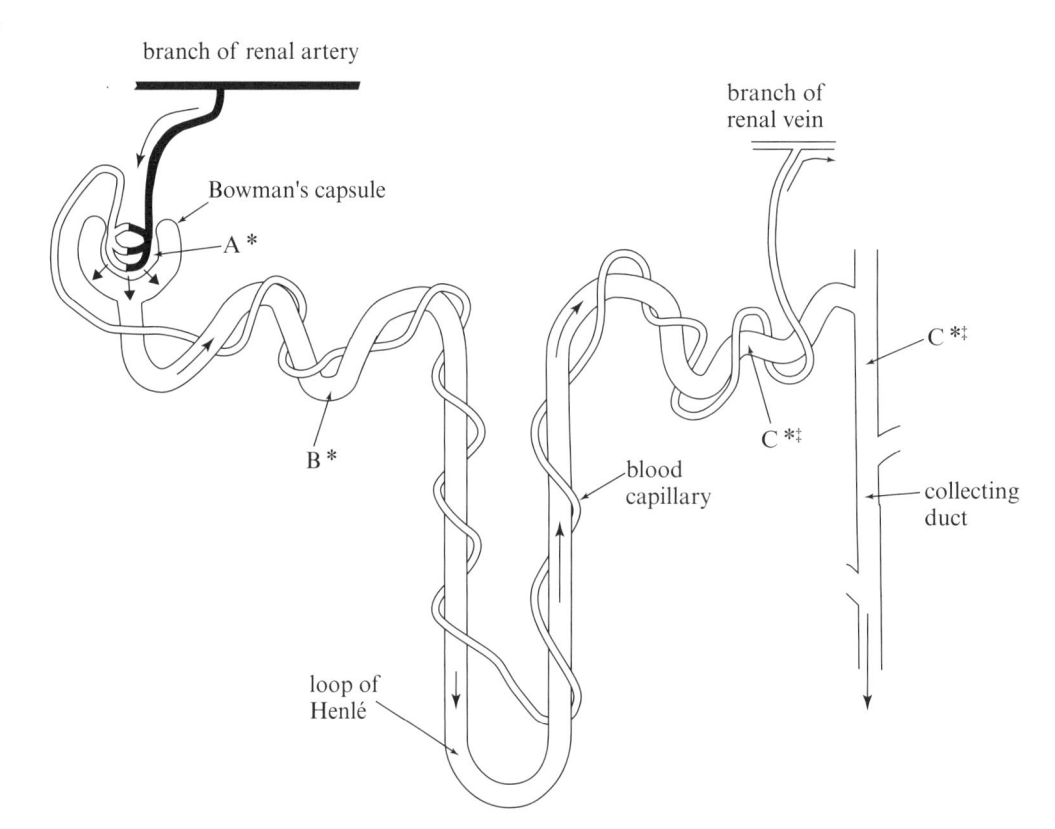

Diagram of nephron showing: branch of renal artery, Bowman's capsule, A, B*, loop of Henlé, blood capillary, C*‡ (two positions), branch of renal vein, collecting duct*

1 mark for each correct label – you do not have to label both positions for C, either will do **3 marks**

(b) (i) proteins/blood cells/antibodies/platelets* **1 mark**

   (ii) glucose/sugar/amino acids/salt/water* **1 mark**

   (iii) urea* **1 mark**

(c) ADH is produced when **a person has exercised a lot***. It **increases*** the permeability of the nephron to water, so **less*** urine is produced. **3 marks**

Total: 9 marks

8. (a)

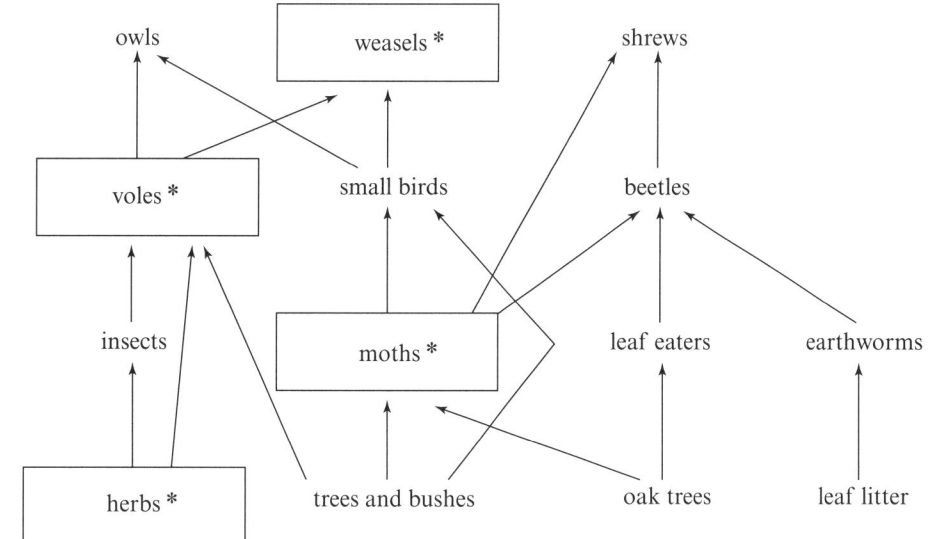

```
owls          weasels *        shrews
  ↖  ↑          ↑              ↑
   voles *   small birds     beetles
    ↑  ↑       ↑  ↑  ↖       ↑ ↑ ↑
   insects    moths *    leaf eaters   earthworms
    ↑          ↑  ↑          ↑            ↑
   herbs *   trees and bushes  oak trees  leaf litter
```

4 marks

(b) (i) oak tree – producer*

(ii) moth – herbivore and primary consumer*

(iii) shrew – top carnivore and tertiary consumer*

(iv) vole – omnivore*   **4 marks**

(c) (i) Pyramid C*   **1 mark**

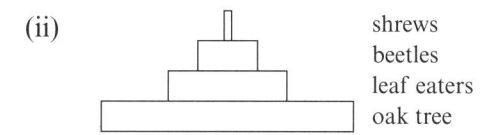

(ii)
```
    ▯         shrews
  ▭▭▭         beetles
 ▭▭▭▭▭        leaf eaters
▭▭▭▭▭▭▭       oak tree
```
1 mark

(iii) It takes account of the size of the organisms involved*.   **1 mark**

(d) (i) If 90% of energy is lost at each stage, 10% is passed on; 10/100 × 500 = 50 kJ*   **1 mark**

> **TIP**
> You do not get extra marks for your calculation, but you should always show your working.

(ii) movement/lost as heat/lost in undigested food*   **1 mark**

> **TIP**
> The energy used for growth is the only energy passed on from one stage to the next.

Total: 13 marks

9. (a) **6 marks**

Letter	Name of cell or cell fragment	How it defends the body from disease
A	phagocyte*	engulfs and destroys germs/can change shape to surround germs*
C	lymphocyte*	makes antibodies to destroy germs*
D	platelets*	important in blood clotting – this helps to stop germs entering wounds*

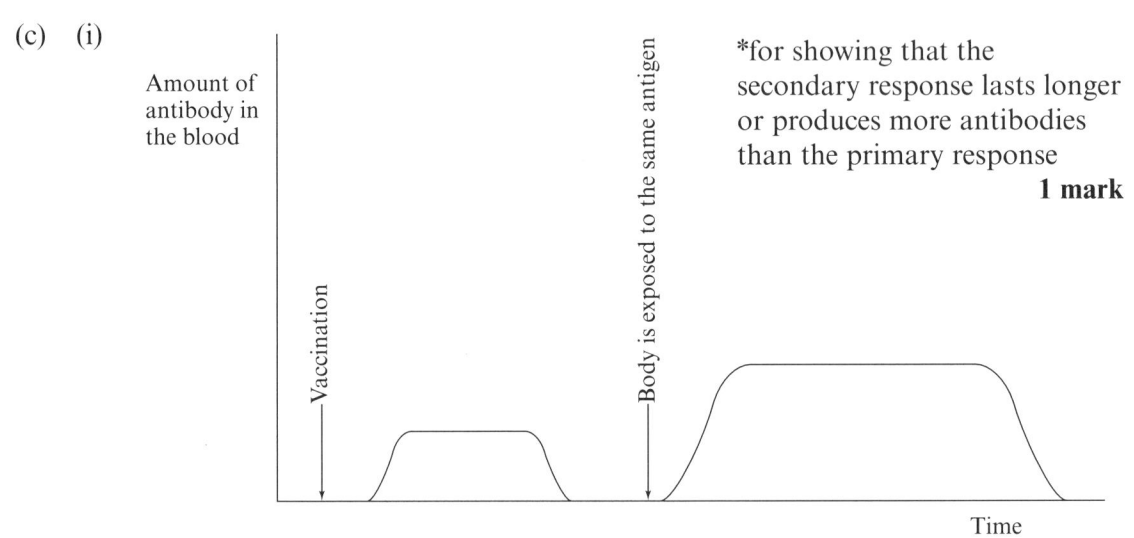

(b) Cell C – lymphocyte*   **1 mark**

(c) (i)

Amount of antibody in the blood / Vaccination / Body is exposed to the same antigen / Time

*for showing that the secondary response lasts longer or produces more antibodies than the primary response   **1 mark**

(ii) Any four points from:

lymphocytes recognise that the antigen in the vaccine is foreign/non self*;‡

they make antibodies to destroy it*;‡

this is the primary response*;‡

when they meet the same antigen later, they produce larger amounts of the antibody*;‡

they produce the antibody very quickly*;‡

this is the secondary response*;‡

the antibodies destroy the pathogen, so that the person does not become ill*;‡

the lymphocytes seem to 'remember' how to make the antibody*.‡   **4 marks**

TIP You will gain most marks for a logical, well-structured answer. Use the graph to help you, and include key terms like antigen, antibody, primary response, secondary response.

Total: 12 marks

10. (a) (i) nitrate*   (ii) plants use nitrogen to make proteins/DNA*   **2 marks**

(b) (i) A – denitrifying bacteria*; B – nitrogen fixing bacteria*; C – nitrifying bacteria*; D – decomposers/saprophytes*   **4 marks**

(ii) most live in root nodules (of peas and beans)*   **1 mark**

Total: 7 marks

Solutions to Paper 3

1. (a) (i) **2 marks**

	Nucleus	**Cell wall**	**Sap vacuole**	**Genes**
Root hair cell	✓	✓	✓	✓*
Egg cell (ovum)	✓			✓*

    you must get the whole line correct to get 1 mark

    (ii) cytoplasm/cell membrane*   **1 mark**

    (iii) root hair cells – mitosis*   egg cells – meiosis*   **2 marks**

    (b) A = nerve cell/neurone*; Function: to carry nerve impulses*; Adaptations: long nerve fibre to connect cells*‡ or myelin sheath (fatty material) around nerve fibre to speed up impulses*‡   **3 marks**

    B = palisade cell*; Function: photosynthesis/to produce sugar*; Adaptations: chloroplasts to trap light*‡ or cylindrical shape to fit together closely*‡   **3 marks**

    Total: 11 marks

2. (a) towards the shoot/right to left*   **1 mark**

    (b) (i) B – 7.8; C – 2.6; D – 0.3*   **1 mark**

    (ii) B – the fan is moving water vapour away from the shoot so that the rate of transpiration is increased*; C – the bag traps water vapour, so humidity increases and the rate of transpiration decreases*; D – stomata close in the dark, so transpiration stops*   **3 marks**

    (iii) it would increase* (because water evaporates faster at higher temperatures)   **1 mark**

    (c) Any two of:
    it moves water up the plant to the leaves*;‡ it moves minerals up the plant to the leaves*;‡ it cools the plant down*.‡   **2 marks**

    Total: 8 marks

3. (a) (i) J*   (ii) bile emulsifies fats/speeds up the digestion of fats/keeps fat globules separate*   **2 marks**

    > **TIP** Bile is not an enzyme. It does not digest fats directly.

    (b) (i) G*   (ii) villi increase the surface area for absorption of digested food   **2 marks**

    (c) (i) C*   (ii) Acid activates enzymes in the stomach*‡
    it lowers the pH so that enzymes have optimum conditions to digest food*‡
    it kills bacteria which may get into the stomach*‡   **2 marks**

    (d) (i) C or D or G or H*   **1 mark**

    (ii)   **6 marks**

Name of enzyme	Substance it digests	Products which are formed
protease	**protein***	**amino acids***
amylase*	starch	**sugars/maltose/glucose***
lipase*	**lipids/fats***	fatty acids and glycerol

    Total: 13 marks

4. (a) women: X^HX^h X^hX^h *
    men: X^HY X^hY *   **2 marks**

   (b) (i) Mr Jones X^hY *   Mrs Jones X^HX^h *   **2 marks**

   (ii) David is a haemophiliac (X^hY) so he must have inherited X^h from his mother*;

   Lucy is a haemophiliac, so she inherited X^h from each parent*;
   therefore Mr Jones is X^hY.

   Sara is a carrier, so she is X^HX^h. She inherited X^h from her father so X^H must have come from her mother*; therefore Mrs Jones is X^HX^h.   **3 marks**

   (iii) probability = 0.5/a half*   **1 mark**

   (iv) Each daughter has an equal chance of being a carrier, or having haemophilia;

   daughters all inherit X^h from Mr Jones*,

   they may inherit X^H or X^h from Mrs Jones*.   **2 marks**

   Mrs Jones   Mr Jones

   X^HX^h X^hY parents

   (X^H) (X^h)   (X^h) (Y)   gametes

	X^h	Y
X^H	X^HX^h	X^HY
X^h	X^hX^h	X^hY

   X^HX^h = carrier female   (Sara)
   X^hX^h = haemophiliac female (Lucy)
   X^HY = normal male
   X^hY = haemophiliac male   (David)

   Total: 10 marks

   TIP
   Make sure that your answers to this question are easy to read: make the symbols you use large and clear, and if you change your mind about a symbol, cross it out and write it again – do not try to alter a symbol. You do not have to draw a cross to get the marks.

5. (a) (i) A – respiration*; B – photosynthesis*; C – decay*   **3 marks**

   (ii) decay (C) involves bacteria*   **1 mark**

   (iii) decomposers/saprophytes*   **1 mark**

   (b) (i) greenhouse effect*   (ii) increased burning of fossil fuels/increased deforestation*
   2 marks

   (c) (i) carbon monoxide*   **1 mark**

   (ii) Any two of:
   it combines with haemoglobin*;‡ it stops red blood cells carrying oxygen properly*;‡
   it causes drowsiness/unconsciousness*‡   **2 marks**

   Total: 10 marks

Solutions to Paper 3 ■ 51

6. (a) a chemical which has an effect on a target organ*   **1 mark**

> **TIP**
> All of these phrases are at least partly true, but you were asked to select the **best**. All of the others have drawbacks, e.g. enzymes are chemicals made by glands; a nerve impulse is a message which co-ordinates body activities, etc.

(b)   **5 marks**

Name of hormone	Where it is produced	When it is produced	Effect of hormone
insulin	pancreas	after a meal	lowers blood sugar level
ADH*	pituitary gland	after sweating/when you have not drunk much*	reduces amount of urine produced
adrenaline*	adrenal glands*	when you are in danger*	raises heart rate and breathing rate

Total: 6 marks

7. (a) (i) potassium hydroxide/sodium hydroxide*   **1 mark**

   (ii) It would turn it cloudy quickly*   **1 mark**

(b) Any 3 of:

   equal masses of soil in each sample*‡

   equal volumes of liquids in the flasks for each sample*‡

   air being pumped through the apparatus at an equal rate for each sample*‡

   use the same end point for each sample, i.e. when the limewater is equally cloudy*‡   **3 marks**

> **TIP**
> The idea of a fair test is very important. The person doing the experiment must control the variables so that only the factor being investigated (type of soil) changes. The key to a fair test is **equal** treatment for each of the soil samples.

(c) (i) put the flasks in a waterbath*   **1 mark**

   (ii) decay happens faster at warmer temperatures*‡

   the decomposers which cause decay (bacteria and fungi) work faster at warmer temperatures*‡

   the reaction is enzyme controlled*‡   **1 mark**

(d) (i) Sample A would contain the most humus*   **1 mark**

   (ii) A – has lots of leaf litter*.‡

   B – crops would not have decayed in the field. They were removed from the soil, so there would be less humus*.‡

   C – plants will not have grown on this land for a long time, so there will be little humus*.‡   **1 mark**

> **TIP**
> You would get a mark for any sensible suggestion here, e.g. if you said B, because compost or manure may have been added to the soil.

(e) small animals living in the soil* **1 mark**

(f) Any 2 of:

repeat the test for each soil sample, and take an average of the results*‡

sieve the soil first, to remove any small animals which may be in it*‡

add a flask of limewater between flask 1 and the soil sample, to show if all the carbon dioxide has been removed from the air*‡ **2 marks**

Total: 12 marks

8. (a) (i) A = adenine* C = cytosine* **2 marks**

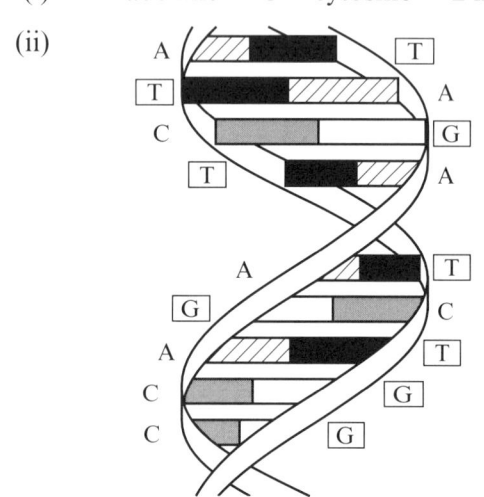

(ii) **1 mark**

(iii) (double) helix* **1 mark**

(b) (i) gene* (ii) threonine, valine* (iii) mutation* (iv) threonine, glutamic acid* **4 marks**

> **TIP**
> Don't be put off by the unfamiliar names of the amino acids in the table. This question is very straightforward if you approach it calmly!

(c) (i) bi-concave disc* **1 mark**

(ii) they pick up oxygen less efficiently (due to a smaller surface area)*‡

they are more likely to block blood vessels*‡ **1 mark**

Total: 10 marks

9. (a) (i) 1900* (ii) 2900* (5200 − 2300) **2 marks**

(b) more people develop kidney failure*; people with kidney failure are living longer before they have a transplant* **2 marks**

(c) Any 4 of:

    the transplanted kidney has 'foreign' antigens on its surface*‡

    the patient's lymphocytes will recognise the new kidney as foreign*‡

    the lymphocytes will make antibodies*‡

    the kidney will be rejected/damaged by the antibodies*‡

    this process is slower/does not occur if the donor and the patient are carefully matched*‡

4 marks

> **TIP**
> You need to think about your answer carefully before you start to write here. Plan a logical sequence of facts to get maximum marks.

(d) (i) To increase the surface area for the transfer of materials* **1 mark**

    (ii) Water*, salt*, urea* **3 marks**

    (iii) It prevents glucose diffusing from the blood into the dialysis fluid*, so that glucose is not lost from the body*. **2 marks**

Total: 14 marks

10. (a) (i) lowers blood sugar level* (ii) diabetes* **2 marks**

   (b) C, E, B, F, D, A* **1 mark**

   (c) (i) nitrogen fixing bacteria* **1 mark**

     (ii) Any 2 of:

        crop plants would grow more quickly*‡

        farmers would not have to add fertiliser to soil*‡

        it would be cheaper to grow the crops*‡ **2 marks**

Total: 6 marks

How well did you do?

How to analyse your mark

Each of the exam papers is worth a maximum of 100 marks. Add up your marks for each paper to calculate your percentage marks.

It is not possible to give the exact mark needed for a particular grade, as these are worked out by the exam boards and will vary slightly from year to year. The following grade boundaries give an indication of the standard needed to achieve each grade.

A* 75% and above
A   68% to 74%
B   60% to 67%
C   52% to 59%
D   45% to 51%

Learning from your mistakes

There are four main reasons why you may have achieved a low score in the exam.

- You did not know your work – the solution to this problem is easy! You need to revise more carefully, then have another go at practice papers.

- You misread the question, so you gave the wrong information in the answer. In future, underline key words in the question, and read the whole question carefully before you start to answer.

- You knew the answer, but did not include enough information to achieve full marks. Look at the number of lines available for your answer, and the number of marks you can achieve for each part of the question. (4 marks) means that you will have to include four distinct facts for full marks.

- You ran out of time, and did not finish the paper. Each exam lasted 90 minutes, and contained 10 questions. The questions were not all the same length, but you should allow an average of 7–8 minutes per question. Check your progress after 30 minutes, and after one hour. If you are stuck, leave the question and go back to it later if you have the time.

If you did not achieve the grade you hoped for, use the points above to work out why – it will probably be a mixture of the reasons listed here. Once you know why you are losing marks, you can start to improve your performance. Remember, everyone can improve their grade by working on their weak areas, and by practising plenty of questions from past papers.

Good luck!

Longman – first stop for study guides!

We hope that you've enjoyed using this **Longman Practice Exam Papers** book. As a leading publisher of study aids for GCSE and A-level students, we have a comprehensive range of other titles designed to help you.

Studying for GCSEs

Longman GCSE Study Guides are designed to help you throughout your course, covering exactly what you need to know and revise for maximum success.

Longman Study Guides have already helped thousands of students make the grade –

"I found Longman Study Guides an absolute lifesaver"
"Longman Study Guides ... were an immense help to me and resulted in my achieving an A Grade!"

– now let them help you!

We have Guides for Biology, Business Studies, Chemistry, Design and Technology, Economics, English, English Literature, French, Geography, German, Higher Mathematics, Information Technology, Mathematics, Music, Physics, Psychology, Religious Studies, Science, Sociology, Spanish and World History. £9.99–£10.99 each.

Revising for GCSEs

Longman Exam Practice Kits concentrate on the subject's core topic areas, and provide students with everything they need to tackle their exams successfully and with confidence.

We have Kits for Biology, Business Studies, Chemistry, English, French, Geography, German, Higher Level Mathematics, Information Technology, Mathematics, Physics and Science. £4.99–£5.99 each.

Longman titles are available from all good bookshops. In case of difficulty, however, please telephone our Customer Information Centre on 01279 623928.

Good luck with your exams!

Moving on to A-levels?

We publish a comprehensive range of **Longman Study Guides** and **Longman Exam Practice Kits** for A and AS-level courses, too!

Studying for A-levels

Longman A-level Study Guides:

Available for: Accounting, Biology, Business Studies, Chemistry, Computer Science, Economics, English, French, Geography, German, Government and Politics, Law, Mathematics, Modern History, Physics, Psychology and Sociology.
£9.99–£10.99 each.

Revising for A-levels

Longman Exam Practice Kits:

Available for: Biology, British and European Modern History, Business Studies, Chemistry, Economics, French, German, Geography, Mathematics, Physics, Psychology and Sociology.
£6.99 each.

Understanding the Curriculum

Longman Students' Guides

Don't forget our **Longman A-level Survival Guide**, packed with invaluable advice. Also available, **Longman Students' Guide to Vocational Education**.
£2.99 each.

Longman titles are available from all good bookshops. In case of difficulty, however, please telephone our Customer Information Centre on 01279 623928.

Good luck with your exams!